A Levite Among the Priests

A Levite Among the Priests

Edward M. Bernstein and the Origins
of the Bretton Woods System

Stanley W. Black

Westview Press
BOULDER • SAN FRANCISCO • OXFORD

Copyright © 1991 by Westview Press, Inc.

Published in 1991 in the United States of America by Westview Press, Inc., 5500 Central Avenue, Boulder, Colorado 80301, and in the United Kingdom by Westview Press, 36 Lonsdale Road, Summertown, Oxford OX2 7EW

Library of Congress Cataloging-in-Publication Data
A CIP catalog record for this book is available from the
   Library of Congress.
ISBN 0-8133-1235-3

Printed and bound in the United States of America

The paper used in this publication meets the requirements
of the American National Standard for Permanence of Paper
for Printed Library Materials Z39.48-1984.

10   9   8   7   6   5   4   3   2   1

Contents

Preface

Few economists of the twentieth century have been as closely involved with the important international monetary events of the period as Edward M. Bernstein. Born in 1904 in New Jersey, he grew up in a family where economic questions were regular family conversation. After undergraduate work at the University of Chicago and a doctoral dissertation under Taussig at Harvard, he took his first permanent position at the North Carolina State College in 1930. His book on *Money and the Economic System* attracted attention in many quarters, leading him first to the University of North Carolina at Chapel Hill in 1935 and thence to the U. S. Treasury in 1940.

As chief economist in the Treasury's Division of Monetary Research, Bernstein was responsible for research on the balance of payments, Foreign Funds Control, and wartime inflation. After becoming Assistant Director of the Division, he also assumed responsibility for the wartime gold and foreign exchange operations of the Treasury. And in early 1942, Bernstein began to work on preparations for the postwar international monetary system. He supervised the technical studies supporting the U.S. proposal for an International Stabilization Fund devised by Harry Dexter White, the Assistant Secretary of the Treasury. He participated in the negotiations during 1942 and 1943 with the United Kingdom, Canada, the Soviet Union, China, and others in preparation for the Bretton Woods Conference of 1944. At the conference, Bernstein served as Executive Secretary and Chief Technical Advisor to the U. S. delegation and acted as spokesman for the delegation.

Subsequently, Bernstein helped guide the Agreement through the Congress over the objections of the banking community. He disagreed with White over the size of the postwar British loan and the draconian Morgenthau plan for a pastoral Germany after the War. In June 1946, Bernstein became the first Director of Research of the International Monetary Fund (IMF), a post he continued to hold until his resignation in 1958. At the IMF, he brought together a notable staff of economists who did innovative work on exchange rates, balance of payments problems, and the adjustment process. He also helped establish the publications *International Financial Statistics* and IMF *Staff Papers*. In 1957 he disagreed with the Managing Director of the Fund, Per Jacobsson over several issues, including the extent of need for additional reserves, and resigned.

After retiring from the International Monetary Fund, Bernstein organized his own firm, EMB Limited, Research Economists, to publish reports on monetary and economic problems. The subscribers included leading central bankers and international financial institutions around the globe. The reports were the source of a steady stream of new ideas for strengthening the international monetary system, including proposals for loans to the Fund from large industrial countries and for the creation of a new reserve asset. These were adopted in modified form by the International Monetary Fund as the General Arrangements to Borrow (the Group of Ten) and Special Drawing Rights. In 1982, he liquidated EMB, Ltd. and became a guest scholar at the Brookings Institution, where he continues to write papers on international monetary problems.

The series of interviews that follows was taped in Washington at the Brookings Institution in November 1983, shortly after I joined the faculty of the University of North Carolina at Chapel Hill. The tapes were transcribed by Amy Glass of the Southern Oral History Program and deposited with the Southern Historical Collection of the University of North Carolina Libraries. Permission to reproduce the interviews in edited form and the three papers written by Edward M. Bernstein on the fortieth anniversary of the Bretton Woods Agreement is gratefully acknowledged. Vaishala Mamgain prepared the Glossary of Names.

Stanley W. Black
Chapel Hill, N. C.

1

Background, Education, and Teaching Career

Stanley Black: You were born in Bayonne, N.J.?

Edward Bernstein: Yes. I was born there in 1904. We moved to New York about 1917. I was brought up in Jamaica, Long Island which was then an extreme part of New York City on Long Island, hardly much settled in those days.

S.B.: What was your father doing?

Bernstein: My father was an insurance agent and later a business broker. He sold businesses--little businesses.

S.B.: Bought and sold them both?

Bernstein: No, he was a broker, he arranged the sales.

S.B.: I see. Do you have brothers and sisters?

Bernstein: I have two sisters--I'm the youngest--one of whom is alive, she's about eighty-five.

S.B.: Did the others go to college, as well as yourself?

Bernstein: No, I was the only one who went to college in my family. There weren't many boys, and we didn't have the tradition of girls going to college seventy years ago. I was the only one in my family who went to college--but, then, I was the only boy in the family. But my cousins did go and, in fact, one of my cousins won the Nobel Prize in physics.

S.B.: Oh, is that right? Who is that?

Bernstein: His name is Arno Penzias and he's vice president of AT&T's Bell Laboratories.

S.B.: How do you spell Penzias?

Bernstein: P-e-n-z-i-a-s. So when I say I'm the only one, I'm talking about children in our own family. In fact, my father had no brothers, and he had one sister. We weren't a prolific family. But the connections through my father's sister provided more boys and girls and they were very good.

S.B.: So, you went to the University of Chicago. What area were you interested in at that time?

Bernstein: I was interested in two things. I was interested in economics because I liked economics and wanted to become an economist, though I thought also of being a journalist specializing in economics. But I mainly enjoyed, for fun, the department of anthropology.

S.B.: Oh, I see.

Bernstein: We were a small group at Chicago in those days; undergraduates and graduates mixed easily and, in fact, after my second year I took almost all graduate courses. I moved very easily with the ten or twelve people who were specializing in anthropology, though I knew the faculty in economics much better.

S.B.: What sort of anthropological interests did you actually have?

Bernstein: Mainly ethnology, that meant the American Indians. I don't think I went much farther than that, a little bit in physical anthropology. I was short one course to make my major in economics; the University waived it. So that waiving . . .

S.B.: Because you'd taken so much in the other area?

Bernstein: Well, it wasn't quite that. I took too many courses in other fields, including history and philosophy. It's true, I had more in anthropology than I needed for a minor. You had to have a field of specialization, and a secondary field. My secondary field was just a little shorter than my major field, which was economics. I should have had one more course in economics, but the University waived it.

S.B.: And your major field, then, was . . .

Bernstein: Economics. I was graduated with honors in economics and in sociology and anthropology.

S.B.: I see, very interesting.

Bernstein: Phi Beta Kappa, too, and I held an honor scholarship in my senior year.

S.B.: What determined you on becoming an economist, or studying that, before you even went there?

Bernstein: Yes, I was an economist, a professional economist since the age of fifteen or sixteen.

S.B.: What were you doing at fifteen or sixteen that . . .

Bernstein: I won the prize in New York County for the best essay on the port of New York. I was given twenty-five dollars in gold. My high school teachers, obviously, were terribly pleased. I had learned a little of the jargon of economics and used that in the essay. We had a very good teacher of elementary economics at high school.

S.B.: What high school was that?

Bernstein: This was Dewitt Clinton High School, the oldest boys high school in New York. The teacher, named Foote, was a Harvard A.B. and A.M., and of course he was pleased to see his student doing so well. Teachers are like that.

S.B.: So you got interested, I suppose a bit, by watching what your father was doing, and then you went on into studying the . . .

Bernstein: Yes, my father once explained to me why gold coins didn't depreciate during World War I. You must bear in mind that during World War I I was old enough to talk in a sensible way. Being born in late 1904, by 1916 I was twelve years old and probably a little more interested in the affairs of the world than boys generally are at that age. We had a couple of Napoleons--gold Napoleons--and my father took them to the bank and we received, in U.S. dollars, the equivalent of the gold content. But at that time, my father explained to me, French francs weren't really worth nineteen cents apiece, but the gold coins were. I wouldn't say this started me on economics, but it does indicate that we talked about economics at our house, about the state of the universe. It was a family in which a good deal of talking went on.

S.B.: And that led you through the course work you did in high school to do the study on the port?

Bernstein: Yes, that was a project for high school students. Everybody in the city of New York was writing on it.

S.B.: Everyone was doing it, yours was just the one that won the prize.

Bernstein: That's right. Nearly everyone was doing it. Let's put it this way, not everybody took economics and there were separate prizes for different counties in the city. I won the one for New York County, I don't know who the other ones were.

S.B.: On to Chicago?

Bernstein: Yes, well they welcomed me there. You know, the University of Chicago was a wonderful place to study.

S.B.: Who were the teachers at that time?

Bernstein: I had Viner, I had a man named Millis, chairman of the department.

S.B.: Mintz?

Bernstein: No, Millis was a specialist in labor. I didn't get any of the great teachers of money at Chicago. In fact, the one I had was simple-minded. One indication of that was a ten-minute quiz on the question 'Which of these would make a good monetary standard?' He went through tin, and copper and iron and wheat and rubber, and other commodities. The question was obvious nonsense. And so I wrote--I was then a pretty wise guy--that rubber would make an excellent standard because it would give us an elastic currency [laughter]. When I wrote that, he called me in and said he understood why I felt the course was too simple, but nevertheless the others needed a course like this and it wasn't proper for me to do this wise-guy bit. It does give you an indication that the class in money in 1925 or '26 wasn't very good. It was much better later on. On the other hand, the courses in theory, in international trade and finance were very good.

S.B.: Viner was teaching both, it sounds like.

Bernstein: That's right. The courses in labor were also good. Millis, the chairman of the department, taught those courses. I'll tell you a very interesting point. As I was very friendly with Millis I got to know Harry Wolf at Chicago. Harry Wolf was a graduate student, had come out of World War I, having lost a leg, and later was a professor at Chapel Hill when I came there. He was much older than I, of course. He was the only man I knew at Chapel Hill from the past.

S.B.: So he was kind of a person to welcome you in?

Bernstein: Yes, that's right, we were neighbors in Bingham Hall and we enjoyed each other.

S.B.: Were there econometricians you worked with or mainly you did trade and theory--those were your specialist areas?

Bernstein: That's right. And later, money.

S.B.: But that was your undergraduate . . .mighty fine teachers that you had there!

Bernstein: That's right. The distinction between undergraduates and graduates was very thin at Chicago. After the second year a person specializing in a field was expected to take the graduate courses. So, the truth was that in anthropology and in economics I took mainly graduate courses.

S.B.: When you got to Harvard was there anything left to learn?

Bernstein: Not very much in what was accepted theory then. A good deal in money and business cycles. Viner is supposed to have said that the best combination for an economist was to go to college at Chicago and take a doctorate at Harvard. I'm not sure it wouldn't be just as good in reverse, and I'm not sure that the same people wouldn't do just as well at two other universities. But it's true, coming to Harvard I ran through the courses fairly easily. I had the scholarship of the Harvard Club of Chicago at Harvard, and I had Taussig as my professor. He became very fond of me, perhaps because he enjoyed my examination paper on theory. I took a competitive examination--essay contest--and won it (I was always good at writing quickly), so that I was the Ricardo Prize Scholar in 1928-29, which paid me about four hundred dollars, or maybe five.

S.B.: That was for writing an essay?

Bernstein: A competitive essay, yes.

S.B.: On what subject?

Bernstein: Well, they gave a choice of topics. The topic that year was trade unions and I wrote one on what trade unions can and can't do. I also applied for a fellowship and I got the University Fellowship simultaneously so with the combination of the Ricardo Prize Scholarship and the University Fellowship, I had a lot of money from Harvard.

S.B.: I would guess so, in those days!

Bernstein: At that stage, this is 1928, I was still thinking in terms of journalism. So I went down to New York to see Oswald Garrison Villard, editor of *The Nation*. He said, "You know, jobs are very hard and journalism doesn't pay much," but he said he'd let me write an editorial for *The Nation*, which I did. I wrote an editorial on a Supreme Court decision on utility rate making. We had dealt poorly with utility rate making and other problems too during and after World War I, much more poorly than we do now, during an inflation which was larger than 1914-29. Well I got twenty-five dollars for that editorial, having spent more than a week on it [laughter]. And when I came back to Cambridge I discovered I'd won all these things. Well that meant that I could make more from my fellowship and scholarship than I could writing for *The Nation*, and I opted to stay on at Harvard.

S.B.: You made an economic decision [laughter].

Bernstein: That's right, I made a straight decision. I was encouraged to do this by Taussig. He was the best of my teachers and I worked with him for three years. I had Hawtrey in money, and he was a very bad teacher but a great thinker. He introduced me for the first time into the way one should think about money. You know his concept of consumer income and outlay, and the effect of interest rates and tight money on investment in traders' inventories, and so on?

S.B.: Yes.

Bernstein: It was a completely new approach.

S.B.: He was visiting that year?

Bernstein: He was visiting. He replaced Young in 1927-28. Young was Harvard's rising star, and he had gone to the London School of Economics as a visiting professor. He died there. In the meantime, we had visiting professors. The first year we had Hawtrey to teach money, and the next year we had Schumpeter. So in my first year Hawtrey on money was a great innovation. The concepts of income and outlay as the method by which money works and the role of the trader in a period of tight money and high interest rates cutting down his inventories were new to me and set me on the right course in money and business cycles. In my second year I had Schumpeter, so that I had very good teachers there.

S.B.: Schumpeter was teaching theory?

Bernstein: No. Theory came only from Taussig. Schumpeter was teaching what would be the equivalent of business cycles. I also had Bullock and he wasn't an easy man to live with.

S.B.: I've heard.

Bernstein: He was accustomed to making very rude remarks and he had small classes in the history of economic thought. We would sit around the class in alphabetical order, eight or ten people, and as my name began with B, I sat next to Bullock. He was a very conservative man, and a bitter man too. He had lost a son in the war and he didn't like the kind of liberalism that was popular in the '20s--although it wasn't really very liberal. Boston had a kind of town meeting called the "Open Forum" and he would refer to it as the "Open Forum, Open Whorem." He also had a strong bias against immigrants and he said he didn't think they had been very patriotic during World War I. I may have been too young to know, but I thought there wasn't much in that proposition. So I once recalled to him in class that New England had a conference at Hartford to secede from the Union during the war of 1812. He didn't reply to that.

Bullock had edited Adam Smith's *Wealth of Nations* for the Harvard Classics. The course in the history of economic thought was one-third Hesiod and two-thirds Adam Smith. I enjoyed the *Wealth of Nations*. I found two or three places where Adam Smith made some of the mistakes on money that became common in the nineteenth century. For example, Adam Smith was very good on the concept that the Bank of England couldn't increase the money supply by issuing more notes as this would lead to an outflow of specie. But he thought it was different if the extra issue was to increase loans to business. You see, he was getting to the 19th century banking concept there. There were one or two other little points like that. After all, Adam Smith wasn't perfect, he was just exceptional! And this impressed Mr. Bullock. In my second year, I spent half my time with Taussig, just writing papers. I took two courses in economics and history, but I gave that much less time than writing papers. I would deliver a paper to Taussig every Friday and we would talk about it, and I would rewrite it. He published two of these notes of mine in the *Quarterly Journal of Economics*. But the most important thing that happened in my second year was that I passed the examination with distinction and quit classes on May 1st.

S.B.: Why was that?

Bernstein: Taussig said he had a job for me. He didn't think I needed more courses. He and I saw eye to eye. His notion of learning was what was called "Economics Twenty." You came to see a professor and wrote a paper every single week. Later the question came up whether I had finished enough courses to qualify for the Ph.D., but as usual the Economics Department waived it. I went to teach at De Pauw University in Greencastle, Indiana for a half year, taking the place of a professor who had a sabbatical. I came back to Cambridge in February and finished my dissertation around June 20th or so. It was the hottest summer.

S.B.: June of what year?

Bernstein: June, 1930. It was the hottest summer I have seen since then and I sat in my rooms at Farwell Place, a little street behind the First Church in Cambridge. I sat in the nude, typing, and every half hour I took a shower. When I submitted what I thought was a draft, Taussig said, "That's good enough, there's no use wasting your time on this--go to work!"

S.B.: What was the subject?

Bernstein: It was the impact of prices and interest rates on utilities during World War I. So I started with a simple concept of inflation, and it was not until later, when I tried to analyze the Great Depression in terms of the money supply and exchange rates, that I really began to understand inflation.

S.B.: Now, what was the main point that you were making in this study?

Bernstein: The main point was that utilities were not earning enough to supply a growing demand. Unless they had enough return, they couldn't expand capacity, although actually they did, in spite of inadequate earnings.

S.B.: And you had to worry about the rate base having its value in historical costs . . .

Bernstein: Yes, or a reproduction cost, something we don't bother with anymore.

S.B.: And so there was some need for figuring out how to deal with that.

Bernstein: Yes, that's right. The question was what would be reasonable from the point of view of the investor, the expanding supply of utility services, and what the consumer had to pay. I didn't go much into the cause of the inflation. Taussig, as you know, was on the Price Control Commission in World War I. And he wrote an article called "Price Fixing as Seen by a Price Fixer." He thought that, on the whole, it wasn't a bad idea to fix prices during the war. I think the main concept in modern terms is that if you allow prices to rise out of hand during a war, it is inevitable that you'll have wages increasing to offset the price rise. Letting market prices prevail in a period of artificial scarcity can give you prices which are unrelated to what you will have once the war scarcity is over. In the meantime, however, you may build this scarcity into costs forever. And I think that's probably the best argument that can be made for price control during an inflation.

I finished my dissertation near the end of June, took the examination at the end of the month, and then went home waiting for a job. I didn't have much difficulty for a very simple reason: Taussig was determined to place me. So, when North Carolina State College invited, or asked me to come meet them in Washington, I did, and they offered me a job as an Associate Professor at three thousand dollars a year, that suited me just fine, three thousand. I was twenty-five years old and thought that was a lot of money.

S.B.: It sounds like you were starting not at the bottom.

Bernstein: No, I didn't start at the bottom. To tell you the truth, although my wife doesn't like me to say it, all my life I've been overappreciated, overhonored and overpaid. Everywhere I went I got to the top of the scale very fast.

S.B.: It helps to have the talent with words, and writing.

Bernstein: Maybe, oh yes, there's nothing like being able to write. Being able to write is a remarkable gift. There's none better, if you can also think. That combination of thinking well and writing clearly and quickly is invaluable.

S.B.: Who brought you to N.C. State? Taussig gave your name, of course.

Bernstein: Well, you see Taussig wouldn't submit any name except mine when he was recommending me. They didn't have any choice, it was take it or leave it. There was a little problem, not about my competence; there wasn't a single Jew on the faculty at North Carolina State, nor, for that matter, at Chapel Hill in those days.

S.B.: In the department of economics or totally?

Bernstein: No, anywhere in the University, with tenure. Well, there weren't many at Harvard for that matter. But nevertheless there were none at North Carolina even though there were two Jews on the executive committee of the trustees: Cone, of Cone mills in Greensboro and Weil of Goldsboro. So it wasn't a question of prejudice. As a matter of fact the dean said to me (this is at North Carolina State), "The faculty wouldn't mind at all, and I don't think the trustees would mind, but there may be some students who aren't accustomed to having Jewish teachers, but if you're willing to come, we're glad to have you." I was perfectly willing to come. I was very fortunate, too, because right after I came everybody began to realize that this was no ordinary cyclical decline, it was a Great Depression. And I had a job during this period.

S.B.: You had a pretty good salary for the time?

Bernstein: I think it was standard. Three thousand was the standard entry salary, though I think if I had gone to a northern university it would have been at a lower rank with the same money. It would have been Assistant Professor at three thousand instead of an Associate.

S.B.: Your money probably went a bit farther there.

Bernstein: Yes, it went farther in North Carolina than it would have in the North.

S.B.: How did you find N.C. State as a place to start out?

Bernstein: Well, N.C. State was a little bit like Chapel Hill, except, shall we put it, not quite as literate. The students ranged from rather poor to a handful of very good. They also had women there--in fact, it was more coed than Chapel Hill--so that the women, who always do their work, were on the whole better students. It may also be that the women were better students because they couldn't go to Chapel Hill, unless they lived in Chapel Hill or unless they were going to the last year.

S.B.: The women?

Bernstein: The women. They had to go to Greensboro, and then they would be in a women's college, or they could go to State and then be in a coed college. I had good women students, while the men ranged from poor to good. The women were uniformly fair to good. I'm not setting low standards; I'm setting the same standards I would today. I taught theory and I taught money and I had my first chance to discuss what I think about money. I taught the basic concept that money had a function and it wasn't to act as a store of value and medium of exchange, that sort of stuff. The function of money was to regulate the production, distribution and utilization of the national income. That was the definition I gave my class and later went into my book, *Money and the Economic System*. The monetary standard is not the piece of commodity you get for a unit of money, the standard is the method by which you regulate the supply of money. What makes the gold standard is not that you can convert a dollar into gold, it's that the monetary authorities can't issue any reserve money unless they have a certain reserve of gold.

This book made a very big impression in a lot of places. One New York publisher, Harcourt Brace, would have been glad to have it if I would add some chapters on banking, but I didn't think I knew enough to write a book on banking. Chapel Hill was very glad to get the book. It got a very good reception, especially in the better universities--at Princeton, at Harvard they used it. Samuelson told one of my students it was the best book on money written up to that time. At Princeton, a man now chairman of the department of economics at Pennsylvania State University, wrote a dissertation on the meaning of the standard in which he says that I was among the first to make the point that the significance of the standard is its control over the supply of money. So it did have a very good reception, especially abroad. It sold out the first printing, oh, in about three or four years.

S.B.: This book was done while you were still at N.C. State?

Bernstein: That's right. It was published while I was still at N.C. State. They invited me to everything, to speak at the civic clubs, and they made me a member of the State History Club, where we had leading politicians as well as two professors. So I enjoyed Raleigh, and I got to know the *News & Observer* well. Jonathan Daniels asked me to write an article on "Gold: An Explanation." This was when we went off the gold standard, and it was reprinted all over the South, and perhaps elsewhere. It was rather reassuring on the whole business of gold. And later I wrote some other little notes for the *News and Observer*, including one on "Inflation: An Explanation." This was about the Inflation Amendment of the Agricultural Adjustment Act. You remember the Act was passed in 1933, one of the earliest New Deal measures. It gave the President the power to change the price of gold, to change the price of silver, and to issue $3 billion of greenbacks. That is why it was called the Inflation Amendment, although really it was a section of the Agricultural Adjustment Act. (The first Agricultural Adjustment Act.)

Later, the Glass-Steagall Act came up. This was either the Banking Act of 1933 or 1934. Senator Glass wasn't satisfied with the Act as given to his committee and complained about the use of the words "and/or." Jonathan Daniels wanted to write about it. I suggested to him, why don't you write an article and call it "Glass and/or Banking." That was the editorial that came out! It was possible too, because I was doing this for the *News & Observer*, to keep it from running off into extremes, now and then. For example, we had a Professor at Chapel Hill named Erickson, teaching English. In 1936 he went to a Black hotel in Durham, where the Communist candidate for Vice President named Davis, a Black, was giving a speech. And people in North Carolina didn't like it at all, including the Raleigh *News & Observer*. So when Edith and I went to visit him [Jonathan Daniels], we said to him, now look, if you want to show that you are a liberal, this is the way to show it. You are a liberal, not just when you support more help for the farmers--that's important, too,--but when you say you don't mind a Professor from Chapel Hill going to a banquet in a Black hotel, for a Negro candidate for Vice President on the Communist ticket. He did write an editorial, pooh-poohing the whole thing.

We now come to how I came to Chapel Hill. The Roosevelt Administration was about to appoint a new director of the Bureau of Foreign and Domestic Commerce. The President had chosen Willard

Thorp to be the new director. But the chairman of the Senate Committee on Interstate Commerce was "Cotton" Ed Smith of South Carolina. In the hearings he discovered that Thorp had registered as a Republican at Amherst (he was teaching there), and "Cotton" Ed Smith said he was damned if he was going to allow the confirmation of a Republican after all these years, so the President withdrew the nomination of Thorp. He did other things for Thorp in return, much more remunerative. He appointed him as one of the trustees in the liquidation of one of the big utility holding companies, in which the fees set by the court were generally fitted to what would go to a distinguished lawyer.

S.B.: It was a bankruptcy case?

Bernstein: Not quite; a reorganization. Later, of course, he became Assistant Secretary of State for Economic Affairs. So I got to know him well.

S.B.: You got to know him because of your utility rate work?

Bernstein: No, I didn't get to know Willard Thorp until I came to Washington and worked on international economic policy.

S.B.: Oh, I see. Well we're back on how you got to Chapel Hill.

Bernstein: When "Cotton" Ed Smith said he couldn't take a Republican, they looked around for someone from the South who was definitely a Democrat and they picked Claudius Murchison, who was at Chapel Hill. He taught money and business cycles and this was my specialty too. So Chapel Hill needed a quick replacement. The department decided on me because I had already written this book on money and they thought they could persuade Graham, who was the president of the joint university, to arrange for me to move over to Chapel Hill. Graham wasn't that easy, he was very fair. Just as Chapel Hill needed someone quickly, so North Carolina State couldn't spare anybody very quickly. The conclusion was that I would be relieved of some teaching at Raleigh, and teach in both places. I would teach money in both places and business cycles in Chapel Hill. And so for two years I moved back and forth.

S.B.: Which years would this have been?

Bernstein: This would have been 1934-35 or 1935-36. This still left the problem as to where I should be permanently and the question was put to President Graham to decide.

Graham, who was a man of unusual qualities, said, "It's very simple to make this decision. Who will make him a full professor?" Chapel Hill said they would make me a full professor beginning with the academic year of 1937. And, even though State would have been willing to do the same, I opted for Chapel Hill and that's the way it came about.

S.B.: Why did you opt for Chapel Hill?

Bernstein: Well, first it had a much better reputation; second, the students were better. It looked like a place where my future would be brighter. So I taught at Chapel Hill. I think some of my students were exceptional. I've mentioned already that I brought several of them with me to the Treasury, and they didn't just do as well as the others already there, they came to the top of the Treasury.

S.B.: Who are you speaking of now?

Bernstein: I'm talking now about Earl Hicks, who had been my assistant. The class in money was very large--eighty students. We divided it into small sections which met one hour a week. Hicks and I alternated. The ones he handled one week, I handled the next. If you take eighty students you can get eight in a group, so each student was in one class of eight and in four classes of eighty weekly. Earl was a very clever fellow. He used to prepare the ten minute exams and one of his questions was, "In a period of deep depression, a forger who forges excellent notes which pass into circulation has done the community a favor." Something like that. The answer had to be yes. He wouldn't take, as the answer, that we ought instead to have the central bank issue the notes, or that maybe the central bank will issue less, because for some reason money was easier than it had intended. Hicks wrote a paper for his master's degree on Alexander Del Mar, published in the *Southern Economic Journal*, which was a remarkably good piece of economic theory on money. He showed that many of the thoughts we accept today were in Alexander Del Mar. He was a mining engineer and metalist, he was against gold and against silver. He was the director of the U.S. Statistical Bureau around 1870. One of his catch phrases was, "The measure of the value of money is all the money." It's the total supply of money that's the measure of the value of money. He had a theory of interest rates which had a distant resemblance to the physiocrats. He thought the interest rate was equal to the rate of growth of the whole economy. If the economy grows at three percent a year (incidently, three percent a year ran through all of his concepts), then three percent is the natural rate of interest. Something like the physiocrats who would have said that it's the rate of growth of trees that determines the rate of interest.

S.B.: Or Irving Fisher.

Bernstein: Yes, well, Irving Fisher answered it. It's the rate of interest that determines how long you let the trees grow for lumber. Incidently, the man who runs the Value Line, Arnold Bernhard, had that theory too: that the interest rate is determined by the real rate of growth of the economy. I sent him the Alexander Del Mar paper.

S.B.: Now, Earl Hicks was a graduate student?

Bernstein: A graduate student. He came from Washington and Lee; he lived in Long Island, in Hicksville. He was brilliant and more intolerant of slow thinking people than I was. That was true when I brought him to the Treasury and to the International Monetary Fund. He gave *International Financial Statistics* a strong monetarist flavor.

S.B.: Did he get that from you?

Bernstein: Yes, he got that from me, but he was even more of a monetarist than I. I was always a qualified monetarist. Hicks never qualified anything.

S.B.: Well, I would have thought Hawtrey would have given you a broader approach.

Bernstein: That's right. I tried to teach money that way.

S.B.: Yes, your book sounds that way too. Who else?

Bernstein: The other student I brought to the Treasury who became distinguished was John Gunter. First, we worked together, he and I, on gold and silver. We'll have to come back to why the Treasury hired me as an economist; but we're talking about the Chapel Hill students. Gunter worked on gold and silver with me. What we were trying to do was to find equations that would explain the behavior of the price of silver, which varied, and the absorption of gold in the arts and industry, and in hoarding, because the price was fixed and it was a question of how much of the supply would be absorbed in the monetary stock and how much by the private sector. The Bureau of the Mint published an annual report on the production and absorption of gold and silver. After Gunter finished the gold and silver studies, he worked with me on how much inflation we would have during the war. Our approach was that the war was a super-expansion and that prices and wages responded to the expansion. The effect of the money supply would manifest itself with a delay, and be more significant after the war than during the war. Our projections stood up very well.

S.B.: He was a good statistical person, it seems.

Bernstein: He was not merely a statistician; he was an econometrician. And he learned it under Dudley Cowden at Chapel Hill. He took the courses in money and business cycles with me, but his doctor's degree was in econometrics. I brought him to the Treasury because I wanted to introduce econometrics in the analysis of Treasury problems.

That is what Gunter did at first. Later, when the war came and we had other problems, I sent Gunter to negotiate an agreement with King Ibn Saud. This was quite a responsibility for a young man; and Gunter did it very well.

After that, he was the Treasury representative in London where he stayed for a year or two. He came back to the Treasury to become assistant director of the Division of Monetary Research. And after a few years in that job, he came to the International Monetary Fund to be acting director of the Middle East Department. He left the Fund a few years ago to become a financial adviser to Saudi Arabia.

S.B.: It pays better, I'm sure!

Bernstein: I think Frank Holzman, who is at Tufts and a specialist on Russia, also worked for me for a brief period, or his wife did.

S.B.: He was in Chapel Hill?

Bernstein: He took his bachelor's degree at Chapel Hill, where he was one of my best students. He was in the U.S. Army in Russia during the war where he was a communications officer and learned Russian. After the war he went to Harvard and became a Russian expert. He was the one who reported back to me that Paul Samuelson said that mine was the "best text on money." So these are among my Chapel Hill students.

S.B.: These are some of your students. What about the faculty colleagues you had there. Were they interesting?

Bernstein: Yes they were good. Harry Wolf, who came from Chicago and whom I knew at Chicago, was a top-notch man in labor. Mr. Woosley was very good in banking.

S.B.: Woosley?

Bernstein: Yes, Woosley. He was very good. Clarence Heer was excellent in public finance. The most distinguished was Zimmerman who was the Kenan professor and a great authority on resources. He left Chapel Hill to go to Texas. Spruill gave more of his time to administration (he was a dean), than to the economics department. Dudley Cowden came after me and he was one of my good friends, and a tennis partner too. Among the younger people were Evans who left to go to the State Department and became Consul General in Bombay. Winslow was another very good man who should have been given higher rank. The Dean of business administration and chairman of the economics department was Dudley DeWitt Carroll for whom one of the buildings is named. He was very interested in getting a good department. He was fond of me and pushed me for promotion. I was a very productive writer at Chapel Hill; I used to write a paper or two every year. Some of them made a lot of sense. I wrote a paper called "Wages, Prices and Interest Rates" for the *Journal of Political Economy*. It was one of the few papers that people remembered me for. When Samuelson first met me he said, "I remember your paper on 'Wages, Prices and Interest Rates.'"

S.B.: What was the main point there?

Bernstein: The main point was that to encourage investment, the gross return on capital must exceed the gross investment cost--that is, interest and depreciation. In a depression, you can get a greater effect on the gross investment cost by a drop in the prices of capital goods than from a reduction in interest rates. The proper conclusion to that paper should have been that in a great depression we ought to give a subsidy for investment.

S.B.: An investment tax credit?

Bernstein: That's right. I didn't come to that conclusion but that's what it all came down to.

S.B.: Mm-hm, mm-hm.

Bernstein: The difficulty in a recession was to get the gross cost of capital down to make the gross return profitable. The paper was also an argument for taking all the depreciation as expensing. When I was at the Treasury and Oskar Lange--you know him?

S.B.: Yes, oh yes.

Bernstein: Oskar Lange was the Ambassador of Poland. He invited a group of people to a cocktail party and when I went through the line I said, "My name is Ed Bernstein," and he said "Are you the author of 'Prices, Wages and Interest Rates?'" [laughter].Well, I loved Chapel Hill, I did. Now, my wife found it . . .

S.B.: What was it you loved about it, particularly? The students and the faculty colleagues?

Bernstein: Yes, the students and the faculty colleagues were fine, and I played tennis a good deal. I was a good tennis player in those days. I was too small to be really very good, but we had tennis all the time in Chapel Hill. Chapel Hill was noted for its tennis . . .

S.B.: Still is.

Bernstein: . . . not for its football. Mr. Graham once walked home from a Duke game with Mrs. Bernstein and me and bewailed the fact that we'd lost once more. We weren't winning games in those days. I loved Chapel Hill, but my wife was lonely there. The problem for my wife was that she was twenty-three years old, and much too young to be accepted by the older faculty wives.

S.B.: You had met her . . . where?

Bernstein: I met her through a friend of mine from Harvard. She went to college at Michigan. One of her schoolmates had married my friend and so when I came up for a holiday in New York, he arranged for us to go out as a foursome at the Roosevelt Hotel, where you could dine and dance very cheaply, at least it seems so to me now.

S.B.: She was from New York as well?

Bernstein: Yes, she was from New York. She came to Chapel Hill as a bride wearing bobby socks. At the age of twenty-three she was the wife of a full professor. There were associate professors at Chapel Hill who were fifty and fifty-five years old, had children going to college, and had problems with money. Here we seemed to be living off the fruits of the earth, reaching the top at an early age. And some of the women didn't welcome her the way the faculty welcomed me. And some of them were proud of their distinguished ancestry. We had no Revolutionary heroes in our family but we did have some distinguished men. One of my ancestors, Samuel Edels, wrote the last commentary on the Talmud, published in the standard editions of the Talmud. That was a big achievement. It even had a Latin name, his commentary, it was called the *Novellae*, the "new ideas." We have a booklet giving that part of our family tree. In any case, my wife was glad when I came to Washington.

When I was in Chapel Hill, Carl Snyder used to come and winter there. He had been the economic adviser at the Federal Reserve Bank of New York. He was a very able but opinionated man. I had just come back from my honeymoon in the fall of 1936, having passed through from Canada by way of Maine, and Edith and I were in Portland, Maine, when the Republicans were holding a parade for Alf Landon. So we decided to watch that parade. Astonishingly, there were very few people in the streets when Alf Landon and his motorcade came through. When I got to Chapel Hill, having had a wonderful ride down, seeing the colors change from red and yellow in Canada and Maine, and getting green again when we got to Chapel Hill, I met Carl Snyder at a party. He said he was pretty sure Landon was going to be elected. I asked him, "Are you going by the Literary Digest Poll?" He said, "Oh no, that's too simple, but the Gallup Poll shows this." Well I said, "The Gallup Poll shows Roosevelt leading Landon by a big margin." He said, "Ah, but you have to take it by the rate of change in the Gallup Poll." [laughter] And then he added, " I am convinced that Landon is going to win, and if he doesn't win I'll give everybody in this room a dinner at the Sir Walter Hotel in Raleigh." And he did give everybody dinner! [laughter]

When we came to know each other better, he told me that when he was at the Federal Reserve Bank of New York he had written short notes--three, four, six, and eight pages--that made a pile a foot high. Would I be willing to edit them for a book?

S.B.: What did you say?

Bernstein: I said if the fee is high enough I would do it! So we agreed on two thousand dollars. Now you must bear in mind that two thousand dollars, if we just go by incomes at Chapel Hill at that time was roughly sixty percent of my salary for a year. And so I said yes. My job was to take what he had written, and put together these little pieces so that they formed a good chapter. I took out his extreme bias but kept his general view, which was very conservative. His view of the

New Deal could almost be summarized as follows: if President Roosevelt had just changed the gold content of the dollar, it would have been enough. We wouldn't have needed all the other measures which he called nonsense. There was a point to be made there and I was willing to make it for him. Snyder was a great believer in inequality; he thought inequality was the law of nature, and what he had in mind was the Pareto curve. So Earl Hicks and I (Earl Hicks got paid separately for being my assistant on this) had to find an explanation of the Pareto curve. One accepted explanation of the Pareto curve is that it is the normal distribution on a logarithmic base. I am referring to the distribution of income.

S.B.: Oh, of course.

Bernstein: The Pareto curve gives exceptional rewards for exceptional qualities and Hicks and I thought it would be easier to explain the unequal distribution of these qualities in terms of major league baseball where salaries ranged from $6,000 to $80,000 a year. Babe Ruth, the highest-paid player, had hit 60 home runs in a season. We found another player, his name was Johnny Cooney, who had played in the majors for about 20 years and had hit only two home runs in that period. But he batted .285 and that was good enough to keep him in the big leagues. Earl Hicks and I decided to construct an equation that would explain the phenomenon of Cooney and Ruth. We started by assuming that there were a number of qualities that big-league players had to have, but not in equal degree for all players. The precise number doesn't matter, maybe there are three or four. But differences in the degree of these qualities are of exceptional importance. Say you have a constant and then you have 'A', 'B', 'C', 'D'--the extraordinary qualities--and each of these qualities has an exponent which measures the degree of the quality. An equation of this kind results in very sharp differences with a normal distribution of the qualities and the exponents. We succeeded in duplicating the Pareto curve with four factors and three exponents, plus a constant. I have no doubt that this is the explanation of the Pareto curve.

S.B.: Now, is this only the distribution of earnings you're talking about or the distribution of income?

Bernstein: Well, we're talking about the distribution of abilities which result in the unequal distribution of income.

S.B.: You know the distinction, of course.

Bernstein: I'm not quite sure.

S.B.: Income is going to include inherited wealth as opposed to earnings which would be . . .

Bernstein: Oh yes, of course, you are right. We didn't make that distinction. I think we just took what we had on the Pareto curve which was on income. These are the statistics I had.

S.B.: Right, right. So, this was the sort of person you were running into while you were there?

Bernstein: Yes. Later this book became a big hit.

S.B.: The book by Snyder?

Bernstein: Called *Capitalism: the Creator*. Wilkie carried it during the campaign against Roosevelt in 1940.

S.B.: Was your name on the book?

Bernstein: No, he offered it, but I couldn't do that as it did not represent my views.

S.B.: I didn't think you would want, perhaps . . .

Bernstein: But I was perfectly willing to have a statement in the book acknowledging my help. I didn't take responsibility for the views nor did Hicks, who worked with me on it.

2

Treasury at War

Bernstein: I was doing well at Chapel Hill, and in 1940 I suddenly got several invitations to come to work in Washington.

S.B.: Nineteen forty was, I suppose, when people were beginning to assume we were going to be involved in the war.

Bernstein: Yes, or at least let me put it this way: the war was getting to be a big consideration in all policy.

S.B.: Had you been writing anything in that area particularly?

Bernstein: Yes, I had written a paper, which is still very good by the way, "War and the Pattern of Business Cycles." That paper is important because it may be the first time that anybody discussed the Kondratieff long waves analytically instead of just assuming these things happen. Kondratieff himself said he didn't know the explanation of this. So "War and the Pattern of Business Cycles" was, I think, a very useful paper. It also took up a question now very important, whether the inflation of the Napoleonic Wars was due to the fact that the government ran a deficit or something else. Tooke said it couldn't have been due to the deficit because after all, if the government borrowed the money, the government spent it instead of somebody else spending it. You get the same arguments today. I quoted Pigou on that. Pigou said that in time of war, the public don't want military expenditures in place of civil expenditures; they want both. That paper, I think, made an impression; certainly the last part which had to do with what would happen after World War II. I was explaining the Great Depression in what is now accepted language, I think. In fact when Haberler wrote a paper for the Joint Economic Committee on the 50th anniversary of the Great Depression he accepted my explanation as the proper one. And this is where I first gave it, though I repeated it in several places. One was in the EMB series and was called "The Nature and Causes of the Deep Depression." Another is an article I wrote for the *Encyclopedia of the Social Sciences*. In that article I have several paragraphs discussing the relationship of gold to great depressions.

S.B.: So this work, it attracted notice . . .

Bernstein: Actually Harry White may have been teaching while he was at the Treasury to earn a little extra money, and he may have been using my book. But, in any case, I got an invitation from the Treasury by telegraph.

S.B.: Directly from White, or one of his . . .

Bernstein: No, from the Undersecretary of the Treasury.

S.B.: Who was . . .

Bernstein: Daniel Bell, a very good friend of mine later. This telegram was read to me over the telephone (it was May of 1940), and it asked me whether I could come to Washington right away. And so when my wife came home I told her, and she said, "Sure, let's go for the summer." Actually, the Treasury was offering me a temporary job for the summer. After I was at the Treasury, I got an invitation then from Galbraith to join him. I've forgotten what he was working on, but it was probably the OPA. So when I came to the Treasury, Mr. White explained what he wanted. We rented a house in Kalorama Road, and we brought up some furniture for our child. And we also brought our servant from Chapel Hill, so that we would all feel at home--especially the baby.

S.B.: Just for the summer?

Bernstein: Yes, just for the summer. But we took enough of his furniture so he would feel at home. We were well settled and I went to work. What the Treasury wanted was this: In 1940 the Senate had passed a resolution called Senate Resolution 40, introduced by Senator Wagner, chairman of the Senate Banking Committee. It was a questionnaire on why the Administration followed certain monetary policies. There were questions on gold, on silver, on foreign exchange, on domestic questions and so on and so on. This questionnaire was prepared by Viner and Hardy. You remember Hardy?

S.B.: C. L. Hardy.

Bernstein: That's right, Charles L. Hardy. He wrote a book called *Do We Have Enough Gold?* published by Brookings. This was a very good questionnaire and it went to the Treasury, the Federal Reserve Board, the Federal Reserve Bank of New York, the American Bankers Association and others. White said to me, "You are going to take charge of the answers." And I had a small office, about the size of this, and a typewriter, because I like to do my work on the typewriter. And I sat at the Treasury for three months and answered those questions. I wrote a volume on monetary policy that summer. The only instruction the Treasury gave me was that everything the Administration did, was well thought out. If something went wrong, it was because of unforeseen circumstances.

S.B.: So how did they receive . . . you said it came to a volume?

Bernstein: It came to a volume because there were roughly a hundred and sixty questions and if I wrote three or four pages on each, double spaced, you would have had around six hundred pages of manuscript. By the time the answers were sent to the Senate Committee, it decided that it had other more urgent problems. The answers prepared by the Treasury never got to be printed. And so they remained manuscript documents in the Treasury.

When I finished answering these questions, I delivered the volume to Mr. White, and told him that I would leave in a few days. This must have been around September 15th. He asked why I was leaving. I said, "I have to go back to teach, I have classes and you hired me just for the summer." He said, "We hire everybody just for the summer, then if we don't want them we can let them go. But we have no intention. . . . You're good." And I said, "You hadn't told me that you wanted me to stay, so I have to make arrangements if I am to stay."

S.B.: He must have had a lot of other things on his mind.

Bernstein: Who, White? He just assumed that I was staying on. Once he'd made the decision in his own mind, he didn't think he had to communicate with me. Well, we got Dean Carroll to come here to discuss my situation with the Treasury. He was very understanding and so was Bob House who was the second man at Chapel Hill. At the Treasury, I had a small staff to work on gold, silver, foreign exchange and Federal Reserve policy.

S.B.: And you were an assistant director at that point to whom?

Bernstein: No, I was just a principal economist.

S.B.: O.k. And there would have been some other economists as well, at that time, up there?

Bernstein: Oh yes, there were others, some of them quite good. The staff was very small and White asked me to hire anyone I needed. And so that fall I brought Earl Hicks and John Gunter, my best graduate students from Chapel Hill, to the Treasury. The next big change for me came in January, 1941, when White called a meeting of the staff and informed us that he had decided to name two additional assistant directors of monetary research--he had one at the time. He told the staff that he had chosen Frank Southard and me. Southard was a professor at Cornell. He had come to the Treasury in September, probably because he had a summer school course. White never asked me whether I wanted the appointment. He spoke about the new problems that the Treasury would have to deal with because of the war. He parcelled out these problems among the assistant directors. I was given the inflation problem and White explained how he wanted the study made. As we left the meeting, I told the first assistant director . . .

S.B.: Who was that?

Bernstein: Frank Coe, I told him that what Mr. White was talking about was just peripherally related to inflation. Coe said to me, "Do it your own way." And so I started a study on how much inflation we would have if we went to war. John Gunter helped me with it. I have to tell you how we did this. What we did was to project what would happen to the GNP in different sectors. I then assumed that the behavior of the economy was a super-boom. And I asked the question how much of a rise in prices did we normally get cyclically, especially when we were recovering from the recessions of 1933 and 1937. And I came to the conclusion that for every two or three percent (somewhere between there) increase in industrial production, we would get a one percent rise in the wholesale price index. And we concluded that that rise would be due to the increase in wages and the increase in raw materials' prices. We assumed that the role of money during the war would not be of great importance because of all the controls we would have. At this time Milton Friedman was brought in by Roy Blough to work on the same question with Professor Shoup of Columbia. Shoup was pressing for more taxes, and Friedman was going to project the amount of inflation. And he came to the conclusion that the inflation would be eight-fold during the war.

S.B.: Eight times the price level!

Bernstein: Eight hundred from a hundred. He also projected the GNP to rise to a thousand billion dollars, though I didn't remember that. Bob Mayo reminded me of it a few years ago. He was a junior member of the Treasury staff in 1941, who later became the budget director under Nixon, and the president of the Federal Reserve Bank of Chicago. Of course, we didn't really get to a GNP of a thousand billion dollars until 1971, and we needed the six years of Vietnam inflation for that. The technique that Friedman used to project the inflation was simple. He assumed, probably really roughly correctly, what the budget deficit would be. He then assumed that a very high part of it would be financed by the banks and the Federal Reserve and concluded that prices would rise proportionately, adjusted for the increase in output. That gave him an eight-fold increase. I thought the large rise in prices would come after the war, that during the war we'd have 33 percent rise in the wholesale price index.

S.B.: Now, you were assuming price controls and Friedman was not, evidently.

Bernstein: That's right. Even if we didn't have price controls, we would have had to have rationing because of the scarcity of many consumer goods. And we would have had to have allocation of materials to make sure that the war industries were not hampered in their production. So that even without price controls, personal saving and business saving would be at very much higher than pre-war rates. Actually, I believed that price controls had a function in time of war and that function was to prevent prices from rising in response to temporary shortages and to prevent wages from trying to keep up with such price rises. After World War I, the wartime inflation was followed by a sharp deflation because gold reserves were not adequate to sustain the higher level of prices. The theme of my paper on wartime inflation was that prices would rise only because of the higher prices of raw materials and wages.

S.B.: The costs.

Bernstein: That's right. There'd be a cost inflation but not a scarcity inflation. Well, about twenty years later I was on a program with Milton Friedman at the University of Chicago and Milton said how glad he was to see his old colleague, Eddie Bernstein. "We worked on inflation together during World War II, but unfortunately we were wrong." [laughter] In any case, my paper was a great hit at the Treasury in 1941. It helped our division establish a reputation for commonsense economics compared to the division of Tax Research and Research and Statistics, the other two research divisions. White was very grateful to me for the inflation study. He was an appreciative division head until we had some differences on policy in 1944. The Secretary of the Treasury was given three studies of inflation--one by me with a projected 33 per cent increase in wholesale prices, one by Friedman with an eightfold rise in prices, and another by Murray Shields with a sixfold rise in prices. Shields had been brought in from the Irving Trust Company as an inflation adviser to the division of Research and Statistics. I am going to use some four letter words; is that all right?

S.B.: That's o.k., sure.

Bernstein: We had these three inflation projections with an unbelievable range. Mr. Morgenthau, the Secretary of the Treasury, called a meeting to which White and I came. White had just told me how glad he was that I had done this study with John Gunter, and how wonderful it was to have a report that didn't just project a couple of numbers but analyzed the inflation problem. It was a large meeting with people from all the war agencies who came to hear the Treasury discuss inflation. Friedman and Shields showed how they had projected the inflation. Actually, Shields' was the same as Friedman's, with slightly different projections of the deficit and the amount of financing by the banks and the Federal Reserve. Essentially, he also set up a table showing the growth of the money supply and the proportionate rise of prices, adjusted for the increase in output. The Secretary said to White,

"Look at these projections." White said, "I don't think there's any merit in them at all." So the Secretary said to Mr. White, "Oh Harry, you always think that if it isn't done by your shop, it isn't any good." White replied, "Shit." [laughter] The Secretary, who was a very prim man, said, "Harry, if you can't talk decently, you'd better leave the room." So White went out of the room and I stayed behind. I then explained to the Secretary our point of view. After the meeting, I went out to see White to report what had happened. He was weeping. White had a short temper, and he was easily upset by the Secretary of the Treasury because he depended for his influence on his close relationship with the Secretary. And though it was unfair to say that White wouldn't have appreciated a good piece of economics done by the other divisions, still he shouldn't have used that language at a meeting with outsiders in the Secretary's office. White and I used to go together to the Secretary's conference. I'd whisper to White what was the really essential point the Secretary ought to emphasize.

S.B.: This was a weekly meeting of some kind?

Bernstein: Weekly, yes. He said to me, "Why don't you just speak up?" At that time I was a bashful fellow. At Chapel Hill I never spoke at faculty meetings. I didn't even speak much in the meeting of the department. Maybe I wasn't interested in what they were discussing at the faculty meeting, which was, quite often the Graham plan for getting professionals out of college football. At the department meeting a lot of the discussion was about the graduate courses. There, I did speak up on the quality of the graduate students and the courses. At the Treasury, White was always very appreciative of my technical ability and the general rule was, if we had a problem, give it to Bernstein. In addition to my other duties, in this way, I became the economist for Foreign Funds Control, which supervised foreign transactions during the war. When the Bretton Woods discussions began, naturally the economic analysis was turned over to me.

S.B.: But before that, the war broke out in December . . .

Bernstein: Well, I'll tell you what I was working on then. When the war broke out in December 1941 I was given the job, among other things (I was still in charge of everything I had been doing before), of economic adviser to Foreign Funds Control. Foreign Funds Control was our exchange control. I was acting director of the exchange stabilization fund. I can tell you little anecdotes if they're of interest.

S.B.: Yes!

Bernstein: In the Foreign Funds Control, the big job for me began in June, 1941. That was one year exactly after I came to the Treasury. The Treasury, the President I should say, decided to freeze the use of dollars by every country in the world under the Trading With the Enemy Act.

S.B.: Before the war.

Bernstein: Before we were in the war. We'd already applied it to Denmark, Norway and France as they were invaded by Germany. Now, in June, 1941, we applied it to every country in the world with the exceptions of the British Commonwealth and Latin America, but we had a blacklist of Latin American firms who were included in the freeze. Even Russia was covered by it, and Russia was invaded that same week. Nevertheless, Russia was covered by it although there couldn't have been many assets the Germans could have seized, like gold and foreign exchange. In other places, the Germans had seized the gold reserves and with the control of the banks and business firms in the occupied countries they could have seized their dollars. Now under the Trading With the Enemy Act, no American including U.S. banks and business firms, could make any payment or engage in a transaction with a resident of any country under the Foreign Funds Control except by a license. Furthermore, a bank was considered as engaging in a transaction if it executed an order of a person in a frozen country to transfer funds. We had all sorts of unusual transactions coming up, and I enjoyed sitting with the committee on Foreign Funds Control. John Pehle, my friend and colleague, a lawyer, was assistant to the Secretary of the Treasury, and director of the Foreign Funds Control, with an interdepartmental board on policy divisions.

S.B.: And you were an adviser to that group?

Bernstein: I was an adviser to Foreign Funds Control and I sat with the interdepartmental board. The board consisted of Ed Foley, who was the General Counsel of the Treasury, as chairman; Dean Acheson, Assistant Secretary of State, as the second man; and Francis Shea, Assistant Attorney General, as the third. It was a great education to sit with the Board when they discussed such sensitive questions as what do we do about Japanese ships coming to San Francisco who want to buy oil, and similar problems involving other countries. At the time we extended the Foreign Funds Control in June 1941, the Treasury also decided to take a census of foreign-owned property in the United States. The man we chose to supervise it was a long-time civil servant, but he didn't know how to go about it, although we had hired him especially for this. So at the last minute I was brought in to supervise the census.

First I had to decide what we wanted to know about the foreign-owned property and who would have to report it. I had to devise the forms and to consult with the banks and business firms on what we expected them to do. It was a dual reporting system. A resident of the United States had to report any foreign owned property that he held. The banks had to report deposits and custody accounts. Companies had to report the stocks and bonds that they issued if they were registered in the name of a non-resident. And people who had come to the United States from countries covered by the freezing order were regarded as under the Foreign Funds Control and they had to report for themselves, so we had to bring all these things together. John Gunter became my assistant on collecting and collating the census reports, so that I didn't have to spend all my time on that. I'll tell you a couple of stories.

The Foreign Funds Control not only worked on blocking the assets in this country that could be seized by Germany, but also applied under the Trading with the Enemy Act to all transactions involving various countries, including Japan. I had a very good time with Foreign Funds Control, but there wasn't much to do with the Stabilization Fund. It didn't really occupy much of my time. But a couple of stories are helpful on this.

Around 1943, a man came to see me and said he was the Treasurer of Aramco and that the State Department had told him that I was the man to see. I said, "I'm glad to see you. Now what do you want to see me about?" He said they were having difficulty in paying the workers in the oil fields in Saudi Arabia. The only currency in the country is silver rials. I asked him, why didn't they buy the rials from the King or his Treasury and they explained that the only thing they could get was silver rials and there wasn't any paper money because Ibn Saud was a close believer in the literal statements of the Koran, and they seemed to imply that you can't have paper money. Well I looked in a handbook I kept in my desk, *All the World's Money*, and found that there was a very good reason why there weren't any silver rials. It had the lowest melting point of any coin in the whole world, for a silver coin. It was, in fact, the size of the old traditional rupee, before the rupee was itself steadily devalued. And it was just loaded with silver, It probably had a melting point of around 80 cents. Now in the United States, at that time, silver was selling for around 64 cents an ounce, the war having brought it up from 35 cents to 64 cents, but that was an arbitrary price that was set by the Treasury. In India, Iran and other Middle East countries silver was over $1.00 an ounce. So that rials were worth more as silver than as money.

I told him I would like to think about this and I would let him know our view in about a day or two. In the meantime, I got in touch with the State Department and the Secretary of the Treasury, because anything done in the Stabilization Fund is actually done in the name of the Secretary of the Treasury. The Stabilization Fund is the Secretary's fund. It isn't part of the General Fund of the Treasury. The Secretary asked me whether there was anything the Treasury could do, and I said yes I see what we can do, if you are willing to do it. I said we would Lend-Lease silver from the General Fund to Saudi Arabia. We would then borrow the dies from the Royal Mint of London--because that's where they used to coin the rials--we would coin them in Philadelphia and then send them by Lend-Lease Air and give them to the King. The King would then sell them to Aramco. I planned to reduce the silver content of the coin, so that the monetary price would be exactly the same as our silver coins, that is $1.29 an ounce. This gave Saudi Arabia a 50% seigniorage even at the market price we had set then for silver. The King undertook to sell the rials at the official exchange rate and take half of the money and put it in the Federal Reserve Bank of New York to be invested in Treasury bills. This would be the money he'd have available to buy silver in the market after the war, to reimburse us.

Well, the State Department was delighted with this, our first agreement with Saudi Arabia, and the Treasury was satisfied with this arrangement. We had already Lend-Leased silver to the United Kingdom, to India, and to Australia. All of this silver, by the way, did come back. It was Lend-Leased to them to produce silver coins, the argument being, that the time to debase a coin is not, in India especially, in the middle of a war that the United Kingdom is fighting! As you may know, we had two billion ounces of free silver in the General Fund. That was the consequence of buying up silver at 25 cents and 35 cents per ounce.

I sent John Gunter, one of my former students at Chapel Hill, to Saudi Arabia, and he made the agreement. The King objected to only one provision of what we had proposed, and that was the investment of the money in Treasury bills, because it paid interest, and that's against the Koran. I told John Gunter to hint in a humorous way that it couldn't be much of a sin, because the interest he was going to get was roughly 3/8 of 1 percent!

I had a big problem on Swiss francs all through this period. The problem came about this way. Switzerland was on the list of countries that were blocked. Therefore, they could buy gold with the dollars they earned, and they earned a good deal of dollars then. Because they were getting dollars from everybody, except the Germans. We didn't allow transfer from blocked accounts to the Swiss, but they got the dollars from the British and they got 'em from us. We allowed them to buy gold with the dollars, but we didn't allow them to ship the gold abroad. I had a standard answer for them.

There was a friendly man, who was the Swiss financial attache, who came to see me regularly about this business. I used to tell him, "Look, when Hitler invades Switzerland, you'll be thanking me for our foresight in not letting you ship the gold there. See what he did with the gold in France!" You see, Germany had seized the gold in the Bank of France, and everywhere else. The other central banks, by the way, had the foresight to send their gold out before the German invasion. The French had much of it out, but not all, and the Germans seized what was in Paris.

In the meantime, we needed Swiss francs, the United States did, the British did, for all sort of purposes, and the Swiss would sell a limited amount of francs to us at the official rate. They wouldn't sell any to the British for dollars, but they had to sell to us, or at least they felt they did. So I got a regular allotment of Swiss francs, and I did this with it. The U.S. Government got all it wanted. I gave the British less than they asked for on the general principal that their request was too large relative to what our government got. And then, whatever I had left from the allotment the Swiss gave me, I divided in three equal parts. One for the Vatican, one for the YMCA (this was all for their work with prisoners of war) and one to the Jewish Joint Distribution Committee, for whatever work they had to do.

We had an Assistant Secretary of the Treasury named Sullivan, later he was the Secretary of the Navy and Charlie Morrow had some documents signed by him, when Charlie was in the Navy. I used to let John Sullivan tell the papal legate in Washington that he had the Swiss money for them. I notified the others myself. The allotments were a very good prize because the Swiss weren't supporting the dollar rate for Swiss francs, and the Swiss franc went to 42 or 43 cents for remittances. They were prepared to take dollars at the official rate for tourism and for U.S. imports. It's very interesting that immediately after the war, before the Swiss gold was released and the dual rate [still] existed, an American could travel to Switzerland, present his dollars with his passport and get Swiss francs for it, and at the same window sell the Swiss francs back again for dollars at the premium price.

S.B.: What was the official rate then?

Bernstein: The official rate would have been around 21 cents or 22 cents. It was really a 100% premium. So our allotments to the religious groups and to the British were really very helpful to them.

In 1944, around Christmas time, the Swiss attache came to see me. He said that he wanted a great favor from me. I said that I was always glad to do a favor for Switzerland. "What is the favor?" He said Hitler wants to give each prisoner of war a gift of $25 for Christmas, and would we be willing to allow this to be done and to sell the dollars for this purpose? I said to him, I knew one thing for certain. We would be glad to have the prisoners of war get a gift from Hitler or from anybody else. We weren't going to spoil their Christmas! As for giving the dollars for the Swiss francs, I asked how much would they need? When he told me, I had a real count of the number of prisoners of war. It turned out, I've forgotten how many there were, but the sum of money, $25 for 300,000 or 400,000 prisoners, didn't involve very much money, maybe 10 million dollars. Their concept was that they would sell the Swiss francs to us to get the dollars.

Well, we made that transaction so that we had an additional $10 million of Swiss francs for allotment. Then I said to him, "We've done you a favor, why don't you do something about the exchange rate in the market? It is a disgrace to your country and to ours. It reflects on us, and it reflects on you, too. It makes you seem as if you are grubbing the last penny from Americans who are engaged in a great war," and so on. He said, "What would you like us to do?" I said, "Sell enough Swiss francs in the market to bring the rate down." He said, "I will ask my government whether they will do it. But you know they object very much to accumulating dollars because you don't let us ship the gold abroad." I gave him the same old story and then told him, "If you can buy the gold, we'll keep it in safe-keeping, and believe me, it is a lot safer at the Federal Reserve Bank of New York that it would be at the Swiss National Bank--safer for you!"

Well, they agreed to use another $10 million of Swiss francs to bring down the exchange rate. They did not want to enter into our markets, but they would sell the francs to us. I said, "If that's the way you feel about it, the Federal Reserve Bank in New York will be our agent to receive about 40-50 million Swiss francs, which they will sell in the market." The Federal Reserve sold the francs in the market, and it brought the rate down to around 29 cents from 42 cents. The Swiss attache came to see me a day or two later and asked how I liked what had been done. I said, "I liked it, as far as it went." He asked me what I meant by that. I said, "The rate went to 29 cents, but I would have liked it much better if it had gone to 21 cents." Then he said to me, "There was a big profit from the transaction, wasn't there?" I told him there was a profit. He said, "Maybe it ought to be used for a humanitarian purpose like the International Red Cross?" I said, "That's a very good idea. You can sell more Swiss francs and give the profits to the Red Cross!" He said, "I mean the profits you made!" "Oh!", I said to him, "That's very difficult. Once the money gets into the U.S. Treasury, it takes an Act of Congress to get it out!" Well, that stopped him right away! [laughter] You can see I had some fun with Swiss francs.

Then I got into the gold-sale business. Until 1972-73, I was the biggest seller of gold in free markets in the world. I sold gold in India, Egypt, and in Persia (Iran)--acting for the U.S. Government.

The way it happened was this. First, White was away, he wasn't at his best. The British Treasury Representative . . . . The British now had a permanent Assistant Secretary of the Treasury, one of the type of Asst. Secretaries there--or Secretary, whatever it may be--represents a Civil Service job. And he later was the head of the whole Civil Service, Sir Frederick Phillips. Naturally he was from Cambridge, and naturally he had won the first prize in mathematics. He was first Wrangler. That's how he got to the Treasury and later became head of the Civil Service. He was here during the war and he had with him an assistant named Playfair. Later Dennis Robertson replaced Playfair and was the Number 2 man for the British Treasury. Their office was not at the Embassy; it was in the Willard Hotel, only two blocks from the U.S. Treasury. Sir Frederick Phillips telephoned me and said that he would like to talk to me about a plan that he had just been asked to convey to the U.S. Treasury.

The problem was this: The British were having great difficulty in persuading the Indians, the Egyptians and the Persians to keep taking Sterling for local currency, which the British needed to pay for their military costs. I understood the problem.

As these countries could not use the sterling to pay for imports at that time, because there was no shipping, so the military expenditures were causing inflation, a burden to them and also to us. The British felt that if we and they sold gold in these countries, we could get a big premium over the official price and it would divert money that would otherwise have been spent on goods and intensified the inflation. The sale of gold would make it more acceptable to these countries to accept sterling. After all, gold is a very attractive asset for hoarders in the Far East and the Middle East.

I told Sir Frederick that first I would write a little note for our Treasury, and then we would let him know in a day or two whether we would join in the gold sales. Well, the Treasury was pleased, but White said to me, "Remember that when you are representing the Treasury, it doesn't matter who it is who wants to see you, he comes to your office, not you to his office." That's the last time I ever left the Treasury to talk to the British or any other foreigners. White had a very strong sense of what was proper. The dignity of the U.S. Treasury was at stake here and I oughtn't to have gone over there. But we did decide to join in the plan and I was in charge of it as a transaction of the Stabilization Fund.

We sold the gold at a 100% premium, at around $70.00/ounce in local currencies. Our Army bought the currencies at par. In form the Stabilization Fund made a large profit, although actually the U.S.

Government was saved from buying the inflated currencies at the official rate. The amounts involved were maybe 200 or 300 million dollars.

At this time White wanted to send one of his staff, Irving S. Friedman, to China, but he thought the Chinese would regard this as an indication of distrust in the way they were using the money the United States had lent them. And that is what White really had in mind. But if I sent Friedman to India, he could stop off in China, as if it were merely a by-product of a more important mission. I couldn't say no to White, and his man went to India and China. When he came back, he wrote a report for me on the gold market in Bombay. He reported that India was about to enter the marriage season and this was the best time to sell gold. So I agreed, that I would sell somewhat more gold than I would ordinarily have sold.

We sold the gold this way: The Bank of England got instructions from us that we were prepared to sell so much, based on our need for the local currencies. They sold twice as much--they took half and we took half. I was not prepared to pass judgement on what the price in rupees should be, but if the Bank of England was willing to take the price, I could always defend what I'm doing. We got the same price as the Bank of England and as gold was a much scarcer commodity to them, certainly for rupees, than it was for us, it was a reasonable arrangement for everyone--the United States, Britain and India.

After I got the report, I told the Bank of England they could sell a little extra gold this time, maybe another 10 or 12 million dollars. The Bank of England did that and transferred the rupees to the Treasury. Imagine my shock when I got a notice from the Army two days later that they would not need any more rupees, because the Army had entered into a reverse Lend-Lease agreement without notifying me that they were planning it! Therefore, they would not be buying rupees from me anymore. Well I was horrified to think that I had sold $10 million dollars of gold for inconvertible currency that I could not use. The first thing I did when I got this news was to go home. The only reason I went home was because I didn't want anybody at the Treasury to ask me questions before I had decided what to do.

S.B.: Because you were going to have to swallow those rupees?

Bernstein: I was going to have to find some way of dealing with this problem! I went home, and I tossed all night on this problem. And finally after a sleepless night, I decided there was only one thing to do, and that was to call in the British Treasury representative (who was then Lord Brand) and tell him that for various reasons I couldn't take the last allotment and would the Bank of England please take it for its own account, and we would take a bit more of the sales in Persia and Egypt. So that the Bank of England would not sell more of their own gold than they wanted to. Incidentally, I also got the Bank of England to sell gold sovereigns to Aramco at the time when we coined the rials under Lend-Lease. Aramco needed gold sovereigns because the terms of their concession from Saudi Arabia provided for the payment of royalties in so many gold shillings per ton. We had no sovereigns and the British were reluctant to sell gold to Aramco. I suggested that the British charge a good premium for the sovereigns because it can't be important to Aramco what they pay for the sovereigns: I suggested they charge Aramco $40.00 an ounce for the sovereigns and we would sell Britain the gold for $35 an ounce.

S.B.: By this time the British don't have much gold of their own left?

Bernstein: Oh yes, the British had gold.

S.B.: Oh yes, they had plenty. In fact, the gold that was being sold in India was half of theirs and half of ours.

Bernstein: Right. But the actual gold sold in five-tola bars (5/8 troy oz.) all came from the Bank of England. Our share of the gold from the Treasury holdings was earmarked here. Gold shipments were getting to be dangerous. The Russians, for example, got certain things free under Lend-Lease but paid for other things which were not on Lend-Lease. To pay for such goods, the Russians shipped gold on a British destroyer. One shipment, on the Essex, was sunk. The Russians agreed to replace the gold. It may very well have been covered by war risk insurance, for which the premium was very high. The Russians used gold to buy some goods from us during the war. The British did not send gold across the sea.

S.B.: How did this affair with the Indians finish out?

Bernstein: I didn't take the rupees; the British kept them. Then I wrote a note for the files which was an instruction to my successor. I wrote, "You will have to keep some of these currencies on hand to meet the needs of the Army. When the war ends, the Army will not need these currencies or will need much less than it did before. As the currencies are inconvertible and our non-military needs will be small, we must be careful to hold no more than the Army will want at the next purchase." My successor later told me that the memorandum on how to estimate how much of these currencies to have on hand was very useful, and the Treasury was able to dispose of all of the currencies it acquired through the gold sales. Besides, my successor felt that the memorandum covered him because he had done what I said to do.

When I came back to the Treasury after having settled the rupee problem, I went around to the Under-Secretary, and he said, "I have been looking for you for two days." I said, "I have been around, just away one day and a couple of hours the next day." He said he needed me every evening because at the end of each day, the Under-Secretary of the Treasury got a telegraphic report (just imagine using telegrams then) from all the Federal Reserve Banks on what the balance of the Treasury was that day. In order to make sure that there wasn't any shortage of money he could borrow from the Stabilization Fund, part of the cash balances of dollars that the Fund held. So, at the end of each day, he would come in with a memorandum stating how much money he wanted to transfer from the Secretary of the Treasury's Special Account (Stabilization Fund) to the General Fund of the Treasury, as an overnight loan. I would have to be there to initial it, and as I wasn't there two nights he was wondering where I was, and he had to get someone else to initial it. Well, that's another one of those little problems you run into. Nowadays it wouldn't bother me, but in those days--in 1943--it really worried me a lot. But, after a time I had to give up the work on Foreign Funds Control because Bretton Woods was taking most of my time.

3

Bretton Woods and
the British Loan

Bernstein: Well, work on Bretton Woods began in December, 1941, just after Pearl Harbor, with a short memorandum by Harry White.

S.B.: That soon?

Bernstein: Yes, I'll tell you what happened. In December, 1941, the State Department decided that because we were at war, we had to have a meeting of the ministers of foreign affairs of the American Republics. And we called the conference to meet around January 20, 1942 in Rio de Janeiro. At this conference Sumner Welles was our principal representative. Of course, he was an expert on Latin America besides being the actual working head of the State Department. He wanted to propose a resolution that the Latin American countries would support. Harry White was one of the delegates. He proposed a resolution that the American Republics recommend that an International Stabilization Fund be established after the war by the United Nations and Associated Nations. The resolution was about five lines. The text of the resolution is published in the Report of the Secretary of the Treasury for the fiscal year ending June, 1942.

White wrote a short memorandum of about four or five pages, in which he suggested that we make such a proposal. The concept of an International Stabilization Fund to advance reserve credit wasn't itself novel, though the idea of making it universal was. Our own Exchange Stabilization Fund was already operating selling dollars for national currencies under repurchase agreements. It took in cruzeiros from Brazil, for example, and gave them dollars to be repaid in a short term. I had proposed, in *Money and the Economic System*, that if a country wanted to have an undervalued currency in order to get the employment benefits of increased exports, the least it could do to avoid too much deflation in other countries, was to hold the currency of the other country, instead of requiring it to be converted into gold. That concept is, of course, the way the International Monetary Fund operates today.

S.B.: That's something like a multiple reserve set-up, isn't it?

Bernstein: It could turn out to be that way, with the United States itself holding the currencies of other countries. If the dollar was undervalued, then obviously, that would give the United States a competitive advantage in world trade and we would run a balance of payments surplus.

S.B:: While we accumulate claims on foreigners.

Bernstein: Now, there are two effects that has. One effect, of course, is the direct employment effect through exports and imports.

S.B.: Mm-hm.

Bernstein: The second one is the monetary deflation effect through the settlement, if you have a system under which the country with the deficit has to deflate to the same extent that it loses gold, or some other reserve asset. And I was proposing in *Money and the Economic System* that instead of claiming gold in settlements, we should extend reserve credit to the deficit countries by acquiring their currency. And, of course, that's actually the way the International Monetary Fund works. It takes in the currency of the deficit country and it gives them dollars or some other currency to settle their payments. That was the concept that White proposed for an International Stabilization Fund.

S.B.: Well, was this a bee that you put in White's ear?

Bernstein: The broad concept of providing reserve credit during the Great Depression was not novel. Keynes proposed the issue of gold notes in *The Means to Prosperity* in 1933. The proposal for an International Stabilization Fund and the principles that it would embody were all originated by Harry White. In a number of places Keynes suggested that I was the author, but that's not correct. As I wrote to Keynes, I was just a Levite serving the priests in their holy work. In any case, the proposal started with White's short memorandum in December, 1941. Then White began to give flesh to his proposals. By 1942, he had written a volume in which he proposed not only the Fund, but also the World Bank.

S.B.: This was a project within the Treasury.

Bernstein: That's right. Nobody else was in on it.

S.B.: O.k., he was the director of the thing--he was the initiator of it. Who was working on it, then?

Bernstein: Well, at that stage, I was the only one working with him, although by the end of 1942 I had about five economists to help us.

S.B.: O.k. And you worked out these ideas according to his proposals, basically . . .

Bernstein: Yes. And then we wrote a simple summary of the plan in the form of articles. Each country would have a quota, paying some of it in gold; it would declare a par value for its currency; it could draw on its quota, and so on.

S.B.: This was being fleshed out in 1942, is that right?

Bernstein: That's right, 1942. Now, let me give you the stages. The first one is December 1941, leading to the resolution at Rio.

S.B.: January of '42, I thought you said.

Bernstein: January of '42 is the date of the Rio resolution. It was December of '41 by White, five pages or so. Then the next stage is a large volume discussing the Fund and the Bank. That would have been written in early 1942 and perhaps revised later in the year. And then we issued a short document called "The Treasury's Proposal for an International Stabilization Fund." That's a ten or twelve page document printed and issued by the Treasury. At about the same time came the Keynes Plan.

S.B.: The one you just spoke of would have been what's called the White Plan.

Bernstein: Right. Then the Keynes Plan came to us, and it was a shorter memorandum, not quite as full as it later was. And I asked Gardner Patterson to analyze it. You know Gardner Patterson?

S.B.: Oh yes, certainly.

Bernstein: Well, Gardner embraced it heart and soul, and I had to tell him we couldn't use his memorandum. We needed a plan which required two things: first, it had to have limited liability on the extension of credit by the United States. Under the Keynes Plan, the United States would initially have had a potential obligation to extend twenty-six billion dollars in reserve credit if all other countries drew dollars. And if the original Keynes formula were applied now, the total quotas of other countries would now be about 2,500 billion dollars.

The second fault was that the Keynes Plan did not require much discipline by other countries. Most of the discipline he had in mind was on the United States as a creditor country. We had this problem in negotiating with a number of countries, especially the Australians, who wanted the United States to guarantee there would be no postwar depression. The concept that we need discipline on the deficit country to correct balance of payments deficits seemed to be lacking, at least in any strong form. Their deficits could run on and on, financed by credit from the Fund.

S.B.: The idea that was in the White Plan was that the Fund would be an arrangement to help exchange assets, but would be self-financing in a sense. Is that right?

Bernstein: No. The Fund would give each country the currency it needed to meet its deficit and the country would give its currency to the Fund. But then it would be obligated to repay the money it drew and it had to begin to correct its balance of payments. In the Keynes Plan there was no obligation to repay unless it developed a balance of payments surplus. The main point was that we wanted conditions attached to the use of the Fund's resources by the deficit countries. We weren't going to give countries money and say, "You can do as you please with it." Second, there had to be a limit to how much money the United States would advance to the deficit countries: In the White Plan the limit was very clear. If we subscribe two billion dollars to the International Monetary Fund, then that's all the Fund can lend in dollars from our subscription. If the Fund wants more, it would ask us, and the Fund would have to ask us for permission to borrow from anybody else. But there was no obligation in the White Plan to give the Fund any more than our original subscription. And that was what we wanted. So I wrote a memorandum on the Keynes Plan that made these two points: We need limited liability, and we need discipline.

Once the papers on the White and Keynes Plans were exchanged between the British and us, an effort was made by each side to have its plan the basis for discussion. Keynes and White were very proud of their plans and they wanted the discussions to start with their own plans. The first suggestion by the British was to discuss the Keynes Plan for exchange rates and reserve credit, and the White Plan for the bank for reconstruction and development. I suggested to White not to discuss the Bank at all until we were sure we had an agreement on the Fund. And that's the way it went. The notes went back and forth between the British and us. We would ask the British questions--in writing--and they would reply; they would ask us questions, and we would reply.

S.B.: This would have been during 1943?

Bernstein: 1943, yes. And during 1943 Keynes came over for a meeting of the U.S. and U.K. economists. At one meeting the British had Keynes, and Robertson, probably Meade and Redvers Opie, and no doubt a few others. We had about ten people. White was sick, Berle, Assistant Secretary of State, presided. Berle was originally in charge for the State Department and when he left to become Ambassador to Brazil, Acheson took over.

At this time in 1943, Berle was the State Department representative and as White was ill, he presided and I was the spokesman for the Treasury. Keynes opened the meeting by saying, "We are prepared to take the plan as you have written it, but want to rewrite it in terms of bancor." Bancor was a unit of account in the Keynes Plan--something like the SDR today, except it was defined as the SDR was originally, in terms of gold. Incidentally, in order to make the White Plan more acceptable to the British we took some ideas from the Keynes Plan and put them into revised versions of the White Plan. I think it helped our discussions for the British to see that we were incorporating parts of the Keynes Plan in our plan.

Bernstein: Now, at this meeting in 1943, Keynes announced that they were prepared to accept the plan as White had revised it, but they would like to rewrite it in bancor. I had to talk for the Treasury. I asked, "If you are prepared to accept the plan, what's the need to rewrite it?" Keynes answered, "Because your plan is written in Cherokee." I am sure it wasn't written in as elegant a style as the Keynes Plan, but the Treasury was more concerned with substance than with style. So I said, "The reason it's in Cherokee is because we need the support of the braves of Wall Street and this is the language they understand." Keynes became nasty to me at this meeting.

S.B.: In what particular form?

Bernstein: He said it was just ignorance on my part not to recognize how much better it would be if the White Plan were rewritten in his terms--bancor.

S.B.: So, it became a little personal in some sense?

Bernstein: Yes. I didn't realize it was as personal as it was because I was so occupied with defending the White Plan. After the meeting, Dennis Robertson, who was stationed here permanently, . . .

S.B.: At the Treasury or at the Embassy?

Bernstein: At the Embassy as the British Treasury representative.

S.B.: So in the memoranda exchange he must have been . . .

Bernstein: That's right. He was the one who was exchanging notes with me. He and Redvers Opie. After the meeting, Robertson (Keynes knew that Robertson and I were good friends) came up to me and thanked me for not replying to Keynes in the kind of language he used to me. After that, Keynes and I got along very well, and the British looked to me to safeguard their position on other matters, particularly the loan after the war.

S.B.: Of course, he knew the United States was in a much stronger economic position at that point, and perhaps he was feeling a little amiss . . .

Bernstein: Yes, he knew that in the end we could do as we pleased.

S.B.: And that didn't please him.

Bernstein: No, not a bit.

S.B.: I'm sure.

Bernstein: I didn't really know how hard he took this meeting. Later when his collected papers were published, Walter Salant pointed out to me the Keynes report of this meeting. And what Keynes said was that I was a "ghetto rat," brilliant, no doubt, but unwilling to listen to reason. To tell the truth, if the Treasury had known he had written a memorandum like that, we would not have held any more discussions with him. The Secretary of the Treasury would definitely have said he wouldn't have it. There were critical remarks in one or two later memoranda. But after Bretton Woods he began to speak of how well I had done and how helpful the report I had written for the Senate Banking Committee would be later on the British loan. Keynes blamed me for the opposition to the Clearing Union, and it suited White to have him think that.

S.B.: But after this meeting, you went back and redrafted the White Plan.

Bernstein: Oh, yes, we made some changes. But we certainly didn't change the substance of our plan.

S.B.: You didn't rewrite the whole thing.

Bernstein: We didn't take the Cherokee out! [laughter] It stayed in Cherokee. Keynes had the strange notion that if it were not for me, he would have his way in the discussions. He would go to White and say he would like certain changes. And White, who didn't like to argue with Keynes and wasn't well anyway (he died only five or six years later)--would say, "Maybe you're right, but I can't get Bernstein to agree, and if he doesn't agree, then we can't do it." [laughter] And Keynes really believed that!

Then he went to the Federal Reserve (this is all in his papers) and they told him that they really supported him, but they couldn't resist the Treasury. There's no bigger piece of nonsense than that. The Federal Reserve had proposed that all countries surrender their gold to the new Fund. One of the big objections the British had to the White Plan was the need to subscribe gold. We felt the new Fund should have some subscriptions in gold from other countries as it would increase the liquidity of the Fund. But the British were against this; they didn't want to surrender any gold. Keynes as usual had a clever line to make his point. He said that the United States, having accumulated all the gold that the deficit countries had, was proposing a plan by which it would get all the gold that the surplus countries had. Well, of course, that's not true.

S.B.: It was supposed to go to the Fund.

Bernstein: That's right. The gold would go to the Fund. But Keynes identified the Fund with the U.S. Treasury. Others had the same notion. The upshot of all this was that Keynes kept thinking that I was the one who prevented his plan from being adopted. Nothing could be farther from the truth--I was only one of many who opposed it.

S.B.: You were simply pointing out the points of the Keynes Plan that were not in agreement with U.S. interests, and then everyone in the Government was agreeing with you, in a sense.

Bernstein: That's right, those who counted were agreeing with me. Most important, White was agreeing with me. I'll put it another way: White was looking to me to come up with reasons why we shouldn't take the Keynes Plan. Remember, there was an enormous amount of pride on each side in getting its plan across.

S.B.: And Keynes had a tremendous reputation at the time, too.

Bernstein: Oh, yes. And you must bear in mind too, that the British were well aware that we could have our way no matter what. I forgot to mention to you that White was a little anti-British, and it appears in a lot of places. When the Lend-Lease Resolution (HR-1776, that's the name for the Lend-Lease) was adopted . . . Morgenthau said that he was going to make sure that the British sell every asset they have to pay for their military equipment from the United States, before we give them Lend-Lease.

S.B.: You had to satisfy Congress, which was after blood.

Bernstein: We still had a lot of isolationists remember. Well, he promised this. We set up a group to monitor the British payments, and I designated Earl Hicks to be in charge. I was going to keep control of it. I didn't just trust Hicks, I loved him. And he would do what I suggested. So we were monitoring the British dollar position. The truth of the matter is that the Treasury was not getting the information because of a technical gap in the capital movement figures. You know the series.

S.B.: Oh yes, sure.

Bernstein: The banking reports. I had to reform them. We weren't using the right definition to get the British and the French dollar holdings. Nearly all of the official dollar assets of the British and the French had been transferred to a Joint Purchasing Commission. As the Commission had a U.S. address, its holdings were not reported by the banks as foreign-owned assets. I changed the definition so that dollars held by foreign diplomatic missions and trade missions were reported by the banks on form B. That gave us the information we needed--how much money they had in all of those accounts.

Bernstein: Well, we finally got everything agreed, and prepared a Joint Statement of Experts which we invited other countries to accept. We had tried to give the White Plan a multilateral flavor by holding a meeting with eighteen countries at the Treasury.

S.B.: Was this the Savannah meeting?

Bernstein: No, we haven't gotten that far just yet. We're still in 1943.

S.B.: Can you clarify what you meant by saying that White was a bit anti-British?

Bernstein: Well, I'll give you several of his statements later, particularly on the British Loan. Continuing on the Fund, we got the Joint Statement of Experts out. After that, we invited 44 countries to a conference at Bretton Woods. Before the conference began on July 1, 1944, we held a preparatory meeting in Atlantic City at which we agreed on what would be presented at Bretton Woods. It was agreed that the conference would have alternative statements on what to put into the Articles of Agreement of the International Monetary Fund. We had an agreement on the World Bank but we were not sure whether there was sufficient support to take it up at Bretton Woods. At Atlantic City, the British and the European governments-in-exile informed us that they would support a bank if its lending power was limited to its subscribed capital: That meant that the United States and the other rich countries would be able to make good any losses from defaults of borrowers. There wouldn't be any loss to the investors.

On the Fund, we were going to leave it to the conference to make certain decisions, by choosing among alternatives that did not differ much on the most important provisions. First, we had a statement taken from the Joint Statement of Principles. Then we would have the text the Americans proposed--alternative 'A'. Then the text the British proposed--alternative 'B'. If anyone else proposed something different, we put it in as alternative 'C'. The purpose in Atlantic City was to agree on a series of proposals so the Conference would know the general shape of what it was to do, but would have, still, the right to choose among alternatives.

S.B.: Do you mean Savannah? Or Atlantic City?

Bernstein: This is Atlantic City. Savannah comes in 1946. Still, there was room for sharp disagreement. When we issued the White Plan in 1943, White and I held a press conference at the Treasury. We had about one hundred and fifty reporters from all over the world, and White explained what we proposed to do and undertook to answer questions. One question was, what will the quotas be for the United States, the British, the Chinese and the Russians. Well, White said, having given what the United States would have, he said, "Well, maybe for the Russians we'll have 1 billion, and for the Chinese 800 million"--I am not sure of the precise figures, but they are not essential. The minute White said this I knew that it was a mistake. So I said to White, "Tell them that this is merely illustrative and that it will all depend upon how large the Fund is." I was afraid the Russians would take this as a commitment and try to bargain up from there.

In the preliminary discussions the Russians had been non-communicative. Gromyko was the Russian ambassador. In 1943, he came in with the Russian representatives to talk to White and me. He told White, "They are the ones who will be our observers at these discussions. They'll ask you questions." Then, as we were finishing, he turned to his Russians and said, "Remember! You are observers. You are not to give any opinion of any kind." That's the way we had to deal with the Russians on Bretton Woods.

Now we get back to Bretton Woods. We've finished at Atlantic City, we've agreed on the documents to be presented--all in there in that big volume, and now we are meeting. The conference was organized into two main commissions, I on the Fund and II on the Bank. Morgenthau was chairman of the general conference. White was chairman of Commission I; Keynes was chairman of Commission II; There was also a third Commission for other resolutions.

As White presided in Commission I, he couldn't act as spokesman for the U.S. delegation, so that fell to me. Incidentally, I was named Executive Secretary of the U.S. Delegation at the suggestion of Acheson. He said, "We need somebody with authority to be Executive Secretary of the Delegation. If someone wants to see the Americans and he can't see the Secretary, and he can't see White, we can give him to Bernstein." And so that's the title I got, Executive Secretary and Chief Technical Advisor of the U.S. Delegation. I had a formidable group of advisors. I had Hansen, from Harvard, Upgren from Minnesota, Angell from Columbia. I held meetings with them every morning and gave them instructions on what to do at the committee meeting. The American delegation consisted of 12 delegates, and Ansel Luxford, who was Chief Legal Advisor, and I, who was Chief Technical Advisor and Executive Secretary of the Delegation.

S.B.: Were there some confrontations?

Bernstein: Yes, there were several confrontations. The first was with the Russians who complained that the committee on quotas had failed to give them the quota they had been promised. I think the committee assigned them a quota of 800 million. First, the Russians protested to the Secretary of the Treasury that Harry White had misled them.

S.B.: Was this to do with that press conference remark?

Bernstein: Oh sure. So the Secretary took me and a Russian expert from the State Department--later he was an ambassador to Russia--to see the Russians. The complaint of the Russians was that Harry White had now proposed to give them a quota of eight hundred million dollars, and they had every reason to believe that the quota should be much more than that. The Secretary asked me, "What's all this based on?" I said I wasn't quite sure what the Russians had in mind; they hadn't mentioned the press conference. I said, "White may have mentioned that a quota of a billion dollars wouldn't be unreasonable for Russia, but he may have been talking about a Fund which was fifty percent larger than the one we are setting up today." I wasn't going to tell the Secretary that White had made this tactical slip. The Russians entered a formal protest and we raised their quota in the Fund to 1.2 billion.

The conference really went very well. I was the spokesman for the United States on everything on the International Monetary Fund. I had a good sense of what Europeans, for example, were interested in. They wanted to know what would happen to their subscriptions if the Fund was liquidated. I had the same interest. At every stage I had in mind that if the Fund plan didn't work, the United States might want to get out. And if it gets out, we want to go out with dignity, without loss, or at least a minimum loss. And I also wanted the others to feel that we're being fair. So I drafted the original liquidation provisions and withdrawal provisions. The Belgians, who later provided the first managing director, wanted slightly different provisions.

Our original proposal for liquidation provided that if a country withdrew, it would get back its own subscription. If the Fund was liquidated and there were losses, then the losses would be borne in proportion to the subscriptions. The Belgians said that meant that if they had no cumulative deficit, if they never borrowed from the Fund, they would have to pay part of the losses. I asked them what alternative they would suggest. They said, "The surplus countries, who are the true lenders, whose currencies are being lent, should bear the loss." Well, I thought it over and I said, "All right, even though we expect to be the surplus country, we'll share the losses. Half will be borne by the subscribers, where we were roughly thirty percent, and half by the surplus countries, where we might be fifty percent or more." But my point was, I wanted the other countries to see that we were fair, and this counted for a lot without any risk for us.

At Bretton Woods I was overwhelmingly busy. Though I was Chief Technical Advisor of the U.S. delegation and in charge of the work on the Bank as well as the Fund, I gave little attention to the Bank. Our spokesman on the Bank was Dean Acheson, and his technical assistants were Collado and Angell. All I did was to read a late draft on which I had a couple of questions. This was late in the conference, so Acheson said to me, "Don't fuck it up, Eddie." And I said, "I absolutely won't." Jim Angell went with me to a meeting of the drafting committee and he came back and reported that the changes I suggested were exactly what we needed. Apart from these few suggestions, I had very little to do with the Bretton Woods agreement on the World Bank. I was acting chairman of the Committee on Unsettled Questions on the International Monetary Fund. The last week of the Bretton Woods conference was devoted more to that committee than to anything else.

There was a daily press conference at Bretton Woods. Mr. Morgenthau wouldn't let Harry White handle it, so I handled it anonymously with my friend Luxford, our chief legal advisor, sitting with me. It's just another example of the petty rivalry between White and Morgenthau, all based on who's going to be getting credit for it. Sometimes I'm amazed at how deep this will to get credit can go. Keynes had it too. He wanted it to be his plan. I didn't care about the credit but I enjoyed my role at Bretton Woods. So I held the daily press conference. It went very well. Occasionally we had a disagreement about what I said, but no great troubles. Generally, Morgenthau and White gave me a free hand.

At this time, we did get through the Bretton Woods Conference. There were some technical problems we had difficulty in solving, and a Special Committee on Unsettled Questions was appointed in the last few days of the conference. We had a little difficulty with the committee which consisted of the United States, the Soviet Union, France, Britain, China, and a few other countries. At its meetings, the Russian representative couldn't agree to anything. He had to refer all questions back to Moscow and we were in the last few days of the conference. I proposed that the committee agree on tentative solutions and then if Moscow said that it was not acceptable, we would reconsider the problems. The Russians didn't like that and they complained to Mr. Morgenthau about me. He asked Mr. Vinson to look into their complaints and he told me to proceed as I thought best. Mr. Vinson, later Secretary of the Treasury and Chief Justice of the United States, was nominally the chairman of the committee. As he was busy with other duties, I acted as the chairman.

Incidentally, the Russians had placed a formal protest against Harry White on the quota question, and it became part of the conference record. They did not submit a formal protest against me. What I did was not a matter of substance, but of procedure. Actually, the Russians helped after that by getting quick answers to our questions. Last year I went to a dinner in honor of Louis Rasminsky, the former Governor of the Bank of Canada, who had been chairman of the Drafting Committee. In his speech he mentioned that I had been chairman of the Committee on Unsettled Problems. He noted that from the present condition of the international monetary system the committee had not really solved the unsettled problems.

I would say that most of the drama came before the conference. The drama was in the 1943-44 discussions. I mentioned to you that we had discussions with other countries--the Canadians were the easiest to talk with--the Australians were the most difficult. They and others were afraid that we would have a great depression after World War II. I told you I'd already written an article in 1940 called, "War and the Pattern of Business Cycles," in which I came to the conclusion that post-war depressions were due to the interaction of the gold standard and wartime inflation. The war inflation exhausted the money-creating power of gold standard countries and the return to the gold standard led to overvaluation and undervaluation of currencies, and I expressed the hope that this wouldn't happen after World War II. By 1943, I was already telling the countries with whom we were discussing the White Plan that there would not be a postwar depression this time. The British were also worried about the possibility of a postwar depression, but they felt that the scarce currency provision to which the U.S. Treasury had agreed would give them freedom to deal with a postwar dollar shortage.

Keynes had invited me to dinner after one of our discussions and that was just before he was to return to England. Also present at the dinner were Thompson McCausland of the Bank of England and Walter Gardner of the Federal Reserve. White was not at the dinner because he was ill.

S.B.: Where was this dinner?

Bernstein: It was at the Washington Statler on K Street. The four of us dined by ourselves, but Lady Keynes appeared intermittently to massage Lord Keynes's chest at about where the heart would be. The conversation at dinner turned to the capital control provisions of the future International Monetary Fund.

Keynes said to us that the United States would be glad, at some time in the future, that the proposed Fund permitted restrictions on capital movements. I said to him, "Is that because you expect us to have a great depression after the war? And, in order to strengthen U.S. employment, we would depreciate the dollar, and that might cause a capital flow?" He said that's what he meant. I told him that I didn't think we would have one, and I explained my view that it was the interaction of wartime inflation and the return to the gold standard, at historical parities, and the consequent deflation that caused great postwar depressions. I said that I didn't think we'd make that mistake this time.

Keynes wrote a memorandum about this dinner, and Eric Roll, who was then at the Treasury, told me about it. That discussion was very important because at various times we were troubled by the representatives of other countries raising the question of what would happen if there would be a great depression. We did agree that if there were a great depression and a scarcity of dollars, they could discriminate against the United States once the dollar was declared scarce by the International Monetary Fund. Other countries mentioned their fear of a postwar depression, and the Australians wanted us to guarantee that there wouldn't be one. I asked them, "What do you want us to do if we give such a guarantee and there is a depression?" I suppose they wanted us to assure them we would follow a very expansive monetary and fiscal policy. In any case, the issue became of little importance after we agreed to the scarce currency provision. Harrod mentions this provision as having had a big effect on British thinking.

Back to Bretton Woods. It was a very smooth conference, because everything of importance had been discussed and settled in the two years of discussion before the Conference.

S.B.: There were only the confrontations with the Russians, you mentioned. And were there a few others?

Bernstein: Yes, we had a few other complaints. Some countries, like Czechoslovakia, believed that their Fund quotas were too small. Everybody wanted a large quota in the Fund, and a small one in the Bank, because in the Bank, they were guarantors of loans; in the Fund they looked at themselves as prospective borrowers, rather than as lenders. I don't think we had much trouble there. With the British, we had no problem on quotas, although there was a question about the gold subscription. All of the developing countries were given larger quotas in the Fund than in the Bank. The U.S. subscription in the Bank, however, was larger than our quota in the Fund.

There was a minor problem with Greece on the provision for a uniform change in par values, that is, a change in the price of gold in all currencies simultaneously. Countries were given two days to declare whether or not they wanted their parity to change under these conditions or to remain unchanged. Varvaressos, who headed the Greek delegation, thought two days wasn't enough, and wanted to know why we chose two days. I answered that we thought two days would be a reasonable period during which the exchange markets could be kept closed. To minimize speculation as to whether or not a country would join in a uniform change in par values we wanted all countries to make the decision at about the same time. Varvaressos agreed that this was reasonable. Incidentally, Papandreou, the present prime minister of Greece, was a member of the Greek delegation. An astonishing number of future prime ministers, finance ministers and central bank governors were among the technical advisers at Bretton Woods. They were technicians moving up in the hierarchy.

There were a lot of questions like that and my job was to answer them. Everybody seemed to be satisfied with the answers. And it made an enormous impression. This helped me in my own future career. There were other problems in the U.S. delegation that were personal.

Mr. Morgenthau had always had an ambivalent attitude toward Harry White, and he was jealous at Bretton Woods because more attention was paid to White than to him. The broadcasting companies had already made arrangements for a broadcast at the end of the Bretton Woods Conference, with White explaining what we had accomplished. Morgenthau did not let White make that broadcast, and so I had to take his place. But Morgenthau didn't want my name mentioned either. So we had a panel in which an unidentified American answered the questions put to him by the others. It was a very successful broadcast. I had tea with Mr. Morgenthau at Bretton Woods and he told me how pleased he was with what I had done. Harry White telephoned my wife, who was not able to come to Bretton Woods, to tell her how well I had done. So everything was great for me until we got back to Washington. And there, as the stories got around about how brilliant I had been at Bretton Woods, Harry White felt his great contribution was being overlooked.

By then Keynes was singing my praises as the hero of Bretton Woods, the economist who made everything clear. When Keynes came back from Bretton Woods he was sure that he could convince the New York bankers to support the Fund. He met with them at the Federal Reserve Bank and found he couldn't get them to support the Fund. Keynes was very sensitive about his persuasive capacity. When he came back, I asked him how the meeting went. The meeting did not go well and he did not think much of New York bankers. Then he added: "Do you know why New York bankers are so successful? They compete with New York bankers!"

I got a report from my friends at the Federal Reserve Bank of New York about the meeting. The bankers were uncertain about a number of provisions. And Keynes said to them, "I've been over the economics and Bernstein has been over the economics, and we are both convinced that the operations of the Fund are technically sound." Then they asked about the repurchase provision and Keynes said, "Bernstein wrote that, and it's correct."

When I heard this, I was frightened, because I thought White would hear about it and get the strange notion that I was taking credit for his work. So I wrote Keynes a letter in which I mentioned his speech in New York and said I was just a Levite serving the priests in their holy work, that the ideas were White's; all I did was to dress them in economic clothing. Keynes wrote a very pleasant reply in which he said, "My dear Levite: We priests need Levites just as the flowers need bees" and so forth. It is a much quoted letter. By then, after Bretton Woods, Keynes was very friendly toward me.

S.B.: So White was satisfied?

Bernstein: I don't think he heard about it. I didn't tell him I wrote the letter; I was just hoping that he wouldn't hear about it. But we then had another crisis when White testified after Bretton Woods before the Senate Committee on Banking. When Taft asked him a very technical question, White said, "You wouldn't understand it; it's too technical." Taft really was a very important and well informed Senator and there was no reason at all to say that. So White had to apologize. Then, White was asked whether Britain would need a loan if Bretton Woods was approved. And White answered, "No, Britain would not need a loan." You know, I had the same dread feeling that I had at the press conference. So I whispered to White, "You should qualify this." But he went off without qualifying it at all.

When we got back to the Treasury, Luxford and I had a private meeting. Luxford was the chief legal advisor of the United States at Bretton Woods. We agreed that White's answer would be a disaster if it were allowed to stand. So, we decided to go and tell Harry White that when I write the Committee report, it would disagree with what he said. Incidentally, all Congressional reports of committees on Bretton Woods and later the British loan agreement were written by me. If you read the House report on Bretton Woods, the Senate report on Bretton Woods, you will be reading what I said. So Luxford and I went in to see Harry White and we explained the situation to him. I said, "We don't know whether you are right or wrong, but you are foreclosing the Treasury's option on a British loan. He asked me what I wanted to write in the report. I said, "I'm perfectly willing, Harry, for you to write the statement about a British loan, provided we have a sentence which says the committee heard your testimony and doesn't agree with it." He saw the point.

This is what I wrote in the Senate Committee Report--"Mr. White testified the British won't need a loan after the war. The Committee does not agree. Whether or not the British will need a loan depends on how much longer the war lasts, how much destruction there is, how quickly their economy recovers," and so on. The Committee Report left the issue of a loan open. Keynes wrote to the British Treasury representative in Washington that the Report struck just the right note.

I was present at all of the Senate and House hearings on Bretton Woods. I had the complete confidence of the Republicans as well as the Democrats. One reason was that there were Republican congressmen on the Bretton Woods delegation, and they had confidence in my objectivity. So that when somebody was testifying on a point that didn't seem reasonable, someone on the committee would call out to me and ask, "Is this true, Eddie?" And I would say yes or no; generally it was true. The people who were testifying were well informed.

I was there during the testimony of Randolph Burgess before the House Committee. He was then president of the American Bankers Association and strongly opposed to the Fund. He gave a long list of criticisms and suggested abandoning the Fund or making major changes in the Fund agreement. I thought he was effective, and it troubled me. When he finished, he said to me, "Well, how did you like my testimony?" I said, "I didn't like it at all. You're starting with the assumption that we can change the Bretton Woods Agreement. We can't. We have made an international agreement that we have to abide by. There are things that could go into the enabling act of the United States and maybe we can say some things there that would meet reasonable objections." He said, "I think the bankers would be satisfied with the right changes."

When I came back to the Treasury, I told White and the Secretary about this. And the Secretary said, "Very well. Dan Bell (who was the Undersecretary) and you and Luxford go to New York, arrange a meeting with the bankers, and see what they want." Luxford and I had already been talking about what we were going to do with the legislation. So the three of us went to New York and we met with the bankers at the Federal Reserve Bank. On their side there were Burgess, Sproul, who was president of the Federal Reserve Bank, John Williams, a professor at Harvard and an adviser to the Federal Reserve Bank, and Leon Fraser who had been president of the Bank for International Settlements. We talked at length--all morning, at lunch, and for a time in the afternoon. Luxford explained what we were prepared to put into the Bretton Woods Agreement Act, our enabling legislation. There were important limitations we were willing to have. They included terminating the President's authority to change the gold content of the dollar; requiring Congressional approval of a change in the par value of the dollar and in the U.S. quota; and the establishment of a National Advisory Council on International Monetary and Financial policy of which the Secretary of the Treasury would be chairman. In the end only Burgess was ready to compromise and we faced the continued opposition of the bankers.

S.B.: In the House?

Bernstein: No, in the Senate Committee. Burgess objected to having twelve executive directors for the Fund, twelve executive directors for the Bank, alternates for each. So that was like a pinochle deck; forty-eight in the aggregate and everything duplicated, you see. In the Senate hearings, Luxford prepared a number of questions for

Senator Fulbright, who was on the Banking Committee. One of them was designed to show that the criticism of the number of directors was unjustified. Fulbright asked Burgess how many vice presidents there were at the National City Bank, and then how many assistant vice presidents. The analogy to the directors and alternates was not precisely accurate, but it did get across the point that if the National City Bank needed so many vice presidents, then 12 directors in the Fund and another 12 in the Bank was not too many. One of the compromises that Luxford and I had proposed was to have the same person as the U.S. Governor for the Fund and the Bank to coordinate our policy toward the two institutions. The executive directors, however, would be different. Actually, one for the Fund was to come from the Treasury and the other for the Bank from the State Department. Our compromises were designed to get support for Bretton Woods in the Congress.

When we came back from the meeting with the bankers and reported what we had done, including the proposed compromises to be in the legislation, White was very unhappy. He asked, "Why do we need the bankers on our side?" What he did then was meet with the Republican members of the banking committee--the House and the Senate--and he made exactly the same proposals to them that we had made to Mr. Burgess. I could see his point. It's one thing to look for compromises with the Congressional committees who are going to pass on the legislation. It's another thing to make them with the American Bankers Association. In any case, this caused hard feelings between White and me to add to our other differences.

S.B.: What were these other differences?

Bernstein: In the meantime, the Treasury had proposed the Morgenthau Plan. White said to me, "You're going to be in charge of the economics of what would be a reasonable role for Germany in post-war Europe. We don't want Germany to be an industrial power again. We're going to convert it to an agricultural economy." The first question that came to me was to prepare a memorandum on how much steel capacity Germany should have. I felt that if Europe was going to be short of steel for reconstruction that the more we could get out of Germany, to go to the others, the better it would be. But White didn't want Germany producing any steel at all, even if it deprived the countries that had been occupied by Germany of steel they needed for reconstruction. And he said, "Look, we're not interested in your reasons for having German steel production. We want you to give us the economic reasons for not having German steel capacity." I told White he would have to get someone else to do it. I was out; someone else came in, Irving S. Friedman. Later they published a book on the

Morgenthau Plan, and they waved it in front of me, as if to say, "See what we can do without you?" Well, they did do it without me. But this added to the difficulties, because I had strong support in the Treasury for my view. I had the Under Secretary, one Assistant Secretary, and all of the Assistants to the Secretary.

The last big trouble I had with White was at the time of the negotiation of the British loan. I have already told you how I had put into the report of the Senate Banking Committee the statement that whether the British would need a postwar loan and how much it would have to be could only be determined after the war. And as I told you, Keynes thought the report was very helpful. And now he came with a large delegation to Washington to negotiate on the size and terms of the British loan.

S.B.: Was this in '45?

Bernstein: Yes, '45. It is after Bretton Woods, and I'm not getting along well with White.

S.B.: No, I can understand.

Bernstein: I was put on a technical committee to determine how much they ought to get and what the terms should be--the economic aspects of the loan. White was chairman of that committee and he called a meeting and Luxford and I went. We expressed our views and White didn't like them. Our view was that unless we lent Britain enough money, the loan would fail of its purpose. Luxford and I also proposed that as a condition of the loan, the Canadians had to lend them money, too. Of course, the British had always intended to get a loan from them. Now they could go to the Canadians and say, "Well, we need your money, but we can't even get the American money unless you make a loan to us." I didn't want the premature convertibility of sterling that White wanted as a condition for the loan. He was still afraid the British would use the sterling balances to get an advantage over us in trade. He wanted to make sure that any country that wanted to buy from us would be able to get dollars for their sterling balances. And that is why White wanted Britain to make sterling convertible as a condition for a loan. I didn't think that could be done, but I didn't argue about it at our first meeting. I thought there would be plenty of time for Luxford and me to present our views. Unfortunately, that was the only meeting that White held of the committee to recommend the amount and the terms of the loan.

The negotiations were coming to their last stage and Luxford and I could see that White was not going to let the Secretary of the Treasury know our views. So we wrote a memorandum to the Secretary in which we said that the loan was too little, that the loans would fail, and we would have to go back to the Congress for more money. Later we showed the memorandum to Richard Gardner--that was long after the event. He refers to it in his book *Sterling-Dollar Diplomacy*. When the Secretary got our memorandum, he called Luxford and me in and asked why we had not said all this before. "Weren't you on the committee that gave us the recommendation on the amount and the conditions of the loan?" We told him that the committee had met only once and we were not given a chance to express our views.

S.B.: You had one meeting.

Bernstein: We had one meeting of that committee. Well the Secretary--it was Vinson now--was mad at White anyway, and he said to me, "You're going to be in charge of presenting the loan to the Congress. And you're going to be in charge of all foreign financial affairs from now on." So White was displaced by me, although I had not sought this job.

S.B.: He kept his title.

Bernstein: Yes. He was Assistant Secretary of the Treasury.

S.B.: At this point you were . . .

Bernstein: I became Assistant to the Secretary of the Treasury for International Affairs. Actually, I was in charge of all economic policy, the same responsibilities that the Under Secretary for Monetary Affairs has now. You can see what this would do to White. We weren't talking at all to each other at that stage. I was given an office much nearer the Secretary than his. The Secretary called me in; he never called White. I think by that time, they were beginning to get worried about White, perhaps that he had been a "fellow traveler" in the 1930's. I think that may have entered into it too. In any case, Vinson didn't like White, and I was put in charge of the work he had done.

Vinson was an easy man to work with. He had an excellent mind. He was one of the men that I knew with the quickest capacity to learn. You could give him a memorandum and he would read it, and he'd be able to handle the figures and even the logic. The only man I knew who was better at this was Dean Acheson. Dean Acheson could read a memorandum on economics, expound it, and even dress it up with stories to amuse his hearers.

The Secretary of the Treasury didn't want to have the Council of Economic Advisors established in 1946. He said to me, "It's going to be a nuisance to the Treasury; it's going to reduce our say-so on economic policy." But I persuaded him that we ought to support it, so we did. That's to say, the Treasury didn't object to establishing the Council and even said it might be useful.

There was another thing that happened at this stage. We were now just after the war. I won't go into the tax problems we had. Taxes were very high. The war was over. We had just had the Victory Loan;

the Treasury had an enormous amount of money on hand. At that stage, Senator Byrd brought in a bill to reduce the public debt limit from $300 billion to $275 billion. As you can see, we weren't talking in big terms then, immediately after the war. Well, I had to prepare a memorandum--actually I had Henry Murphy prepare it for me--and in this memorandum he said that if you want to reduce the debt, the way to do it is tax more, and spend less. Vinson said to me, "We really have to do something better than that. Now tell me, what is the debt?" I said, "The debt is actually around $240 billion, so we have $35 billion to go." He said, "What's our cash position?" I said, "Our budget position is very good, we'll have an enormous surplus, and we have around twenty billion dollars in cash now." Well, he said to me, "What's your objection to Senator Byrd's bill? Let's make him happy. We have a big cash balance. We're going to have a surplus as long as our taxes are this high. By the time we have a deficit, we'll have a Republican administration and we certainly won't hit the new debt ceiling until the next President. So let's say yes." That's exactly what we did. It may have been the only time, since 1920, that the debt limit was reduced by legislation instead of increased. Well, naturally it went over very big. Mr. Byrd told the Secretary of the Treasury that he was the greatest Secretary of the Treasury since Gallatin, or since Alexander Hamilton, and we were all very happy. You see, there was fun in all of this. Incidentally, we didn't raise the debt limit again until 1954, well past the Korean War.

When the Secretary had to testify on the British loan before the Senate Banking Committee, I rode down with him and with the General Counsel. The Secretary said to me, "What are they going to ask me?" You know, we always have a lot of material ready on what the Committee may ask the Secretary. And I said, "The first question will be, Harry White said the British aren't going to need a loan, and here you are coming to us to approve a loan." The Secretary then asked me, "What's the answer to that?" I said, "The answer is on page 20 of the report of the Senate Committee which rejected what Harry White said." There was the General Counsel of the Treasury, who was a friend of Harry White's, sitting there while I'm telling this to the Secretary. Of course, this got back to White.

In fact, that was the very first question that the Committee asked Judge Vinson. And he had the perfect answer. He replied, "Mr. White did say that, but your Committee understood much better than White what the situation would be, and you said . . . ." And then the Secretary read the Committee Report to them. "Now we know what the situation is, and we can tell you that this is the minimum the British are going to need." There were many pointed questions. One senator asked, "Aren't you afraid that the loan to the British will divide the world into two groups?" Vinson said, "The world is already divided into two groups, I'm just trying to prevent it from being divided into three groups." Vinson was a very clever witness. The only man I know who was better was Acheson. And, though Acheson was better at testifying, he didn't make the impression on a Congressional Committee that Vinson did. To Congress, he was one of their own who played poker with the President! Acheson was a little too aristocratic for some congressmen.

When the bill came to the Senate, Senator Barkley was then the majority leader (he hadn't yet been elected vice-president, which was in '48) and he needed someone to help him. So I sat with him on the Senate floor. It's an intimate place, and conducive to real debate. Just across the aisle, not much farther away than you are, was Senator Taft who was the Republican minority leader. Barkley made a tearjerking speech about how the British were in great trouble during the war, and how they were so desperate for money they had to freeze the sterling balances and use them for the war. He had the strange notion that the blocked sterling was money seized by the British to run the war. And so now, having carried this heavy burden, Britain needs three billion nine hundred million dollars of new money and four hundred odd million dollars of credit for lend-lease already in the pipeline but delivered after the war. Then, Taft got up and he said he wanted to be as generous as anyone, but he couldn't see how the British needed more than a billion dollars. This kind of argument--I can't see how they need more than so much--came up steadily. I had it on the British loan and I had it later on the French loan where I headed the technical committee on the amount that France would need after the war.

Well, after Barkley's speech I ran out to the reporter, got his stenographic record, and revised it so that it would be accurate for the record, trying as much to keep Barkley's words.

S.B.: The speech by . . .

Bernstein: Barkley. To make reasonably sound economics out of it. I didn't want anyone to be quoting a speech on the British loan that didn't make sense. Well, there's where we were in the spring of 1946.

After the British loan we had the French loan. The French sent a distinguished delegation to negotiate the loan. The head was Leon Blum, the former prime minister who had just been rescued from a concentration camp. With him were Jean Monnet, already noted as the apostle of European integration, and Emmanuel Monnick, Governor of the Bank of France. I headed an interdepartmental technical committee to decide on France's foreign exchange needs. Triffin represented the Federal Reserve on this committee, and it was there that I came to know him and later appoint him as chief of a division in the International Monetary Fund when I became the director of research. The French wanted a large loan, comparable to that made to Britain. As a practical matter this was impossible as it would have necessitated a congressional appropriation. Instead, we planned to use the Export-Import Bank as the lender. The Bank had just freed a billion dollars that had been earmarked for a loan to Russia. The Russians wanted a loan of $10 billion for reconstruction and would not accept the Export-Import Bank loan. With the removal of the earmark for Russia, the Bank had a billion dollars available out of which a loan of $600-700 million could be made to France. Bill Martin, who was then the head of the Export-Import Bank, did not want to make the loan. He said that would make the Export-Import Bank a one-country creditor. With their prewar borrowing from the Export-Import Bank, and the large new loan, France would have had sixty percent of all the loans outstanding. I thought Mr. Martin had a point. If he was going to run the Export-Import Bank like a bank, he wouldn't want all the loans made to one country.

S.B.: So would you have preferred to lend to somebody else? What did you tell him, lend to somebody else?

Bernstein: Oh, no. He couldn't lend that money to someone else because we needed what he had for France. We didn't want to go to the Congress, you see. And we had set aside a billion dollars at the Export-Import Bank to lend to the Russians, but the Russians said they wouldn't take a billion dollars--it was too little. Either five billion or nothing. So it was nothing. They wanted more than the British. Maybe they would have settled for what the British got. We never could get a lend-lease settlement, you know, with the Russians either. Well, I understood the argument that you don't want to be a one-country bank; we have some pictures of it today, where some of our banks have four or five percent of their assets in the form of claims on single countries, maybe more. Not five percent of their capital and surplus, but of their assets. And this is very troublesome. So I could understand it as a banker, but, as I said to Mr. Martin, "Bill, we aren't running the Export-Import Bank as a money-making bank for it's own sake with banking standards, we're trying to run it as an instrument of the economic policy of the United States. Of course, we want to help our exports too. But it's also broader than that." In any case, he couldn't stop it. The Treasury could get what it wanted.

4

The International Monetary Fund

Bernstein: It was at these conferences that Monnet said to me one day while walking with my wife and me, "Who's going to run the International Monetary Fund?" I said, "Mr. Gutt is going to be the first managing director." He said, "I don't mean that, Eddie. I mean who, at the Treasury, is going to run the International Monetary Fund?" He said, "Are you?" I said, "If I stay at the Treasury I may run it. I mean I'd be running our side of it--but more likely I'll join the Fund."

Remember, at Savannah, White and I weren't talking. I was in the midst of the British loan, and I was keeping in touch with the Treasury in Washington every day (we had a direct line) as that was my job. White was busy doing other things. He was busy setting out what we wanted on management of the Fund. You know the British were very unhappy with Savannah. But, I wasn't really part of that delegation; I was there as the principal spokesman for the Secretary. White was being elbowed out more and more as the Treasury spokesman, even though he was doing the talking down there. And at the end of the meeting I heard all about how badly Keynes felt. At the final dinner I had the orchestra play "For He's a Jolly Good Fellow" when Keynes went out. And then I spoke to him and he told me he wasn't happy with what had been done; but he was looking forward to my being the director of research, because he had confidence in my economics, and also in my objectivity, and he was worried about objectivity.

This was probably in March or April 1946, and a month later, in May or June the Fund was appointing its staff. White had long said that I would have to be the director of research because there wasn't anybody else as familiar with the technical economics of the Fund. But when the question came up in the Fund Board and he was asked for his recommendations, he said, "Well, the Treasury has two people it would recommend. One is Frank Coe, and the other is Bernstein. They're equally competent technically and Coe is a better administrator."

I got the story right away because everybody who had been at Bretton Woods was fond of me and they wanted me. So I got the story right away, and the first thing I did was to say to Luxford, "I'm going to tell the Secretary of the Treasury." He said, "No. Let's go see Harry White first." So we went to see Harry White and he called in Coe. I said to Harry White, "You didn't keep your word. You said you would recommend me to be the director of research." He said, "Well, I did recommend you." I said, "When you recommend me and Coe and you say we're equally competent technically and Coe is a better administrator, I don't regard that as recommending me." At this stage, Coe intervened and said, "Now, Eddie, I want you to know, I do not claim to be equally competent with you, technically. I'm not." That took a lot of wind out of White's sails. So, White said to me, "Well, what's the use of fussing? You're going to get it anyway."

But that didn't satisfy me. I spoke to the Secretary, and I spoke to Acheson. Acheson said to me, "You've got a glorious career ahead of you at the Treasury. If you go to the International Monetary Fund where White is going to be the U.S. Executive Director, you'd have to contend with him again. What do you want that for?" I said, "Well, there are two reasons why I want the job. First, the salary is going to be much higher. And second, there is a lot of new technical economics that will have to be developed at the Fund, and I want to do it." When I went to see the Secretary, he said, "That's all right, there won't be any trouble about that," and he said, "There's going to be a cocktail party given by the Executive Directors. You and Edith come with Mrs. Vinson and me." We arrived in his limousine, and we went through the receiving line together with Vinson and Mrs. Vinson. And he said to everyone, "You all know Eddie Bernstein. He's my principal assistant." So I got the job of being the director of research.

About a month later, the Executive Directors called me in and said, "You're going to be in charge of everything. We'd like to know what you think our big problems are going to be." I said to them at this first meeting of the Executive Directors of the International Monetary Fund, "Actually, our problem is going to be inflation. We had piled up all this liquidity during the war and it will ultimately be activated. The assets acquired during the war are concentrated in cash and bonds. When people spend the cash, prices will go up, wages will have to go up too, so we'll have ten years of inflation of prices and wages. As for the exchange rates, they aren't going to be decisive until two or three years from now. When the United States has its first recession, it'll become apparent that the initial exchange rates can't survive any longer. But we don't have to worry--until that time--about changes in exchange rates." So that was my first meeting with them. These views were the basis for the first *Annual Report* of the Fund and they were later published in two papers--one in *Staff Papers* of the IMF and the other, under Gutt's name, in the *Review of Economics and Statistics.*

I had a lot of work on my hands then. The immediate problem was to set initial par values so that the Fund could start to operate. Everybody was eager to get it working by the end of December of 1946. That gave me six months to recruit and organize a staff, and spend a little time educating the managing director and the 12 executive directors on the initial par values.

We had a lot of problems there. Two of them I'm going to mention as specific problems, and then I'll give you the general philosophy I had to develop for it. One problem was to justify, as initial par values, the rates that already prevailed. Nobody was ready to change par values then, and I had to get the economics to justify it. This was made more difficult by exaggerated statements on the long-term effects of the war. For example, a very distinguished Dutch economist said that the loss of the Netherlands East Indies would be a disaster to the economy of the Netherlands, because ten percent of the income of the Netherlands came from the Netherlands East Indies. In this case we had to make it clear that if ten percent of the Netherlands' income was earned by exporting to the East Indies, it did not mean that the independence of Indonesia would reduce the national income by ten percent. The Netherlands could export the same goods to Indonesia or to other countries or produce different goods for the home market.

Then our other problem was on South Africa. I had a woman working for me who was a Greek, and her name was Rena Zafiriou. And she had been helping Varvaressos, formerly the governor of the Bank of Greece and then a director at the World Bank. She was an able woman. But I didn't realize how leftist her views were. She wrote a memorandum to the effect that nobody can say what the initial par value of South Africa's currency should be, or how long any par value could last, because with apartheid South Africa might not be able to keep the blacks working in the gold mines. This really put me in a terrible bind. For one thing, I thought the statement was overdrawn. On the other hand, I was starting with a staff whom I had told to write good imaginative economics, and to leave it to me to get the Fund's directors to accept their conclusions.

Well, I didn't want to take the reference to apartheid out. I went to the Board with it, and, not surprisingly, the British jumped on me. It was irrelevant. I said that if the par value would be affected by a breakdown in the gold mining industry, then this is a relevant point. But Harry White didn't support me even though he was supposed to be a radical, and my friend Rasminsky, who later became governor of the bank of Canada said to me, "You really went farther than you should. It would have been much more sensible to drop it." Well, I knew it would have been more sensible to drop it, but I had this problem of assuring my staff of their freedom to say what they think. Apart from the South Africa paper, everybody was overwhelmingly pleased with our par value memoranda. They were objective, they were frank.

S.B.: And there was one for each country?

Bernstein: One for each country that was a member of the Fund. Forty-four. And then I wrote a memorandum which got me into a bit of trouble. It said, the initial par values are correct, though we must recognize two things: First, many of the par values are going to have to be changed on the first recession in the United States and we are going to have a normal recession in two or three years. And then I said, quite apart from that, there are several countries in which the exchange rate, even though it's satisfactory now, won't be satisfactory for very long. And I named the countries. I had Mexico in there and I had France in there, and others. This was a mistake. I was undermining confidence in these exchange rates. It would have been wiser not to have issued the memorandum.

Now we had the initial par values, and I wrote a memorandum to explain the economics of the initial par values. I said that we were in a period in which the function of an exchange rate can only be partially fulfilled. The function of an exchange rate, to put it simply, is to stimulate exports and to restrain imports. And if you have the right exchange rate you will be restraining the imports of goods and services, with an allowance being made for services and capital transactions.

Now, at this time there was no way by which these countries, whose capacity to produce had been destroyed, who were desperate for additional resources to reconstruct, could use the exchange rate to restrict their imports. So the thing that we want to look at was whether the exchange rate would allow a recovery in exports. And that is the function of the exchange rate we ought to emphasize now. They will be getting aid from the United States and other countries to finance their imports. We're not really trying to restrict their imports to the level that they can pay for with their exports. But when the time comes when they have difficulty in exporting, that is at the first U.S. recession, we can change the initial par values.

This paper was used as a speech by the Managing Director, Gutt, at Harvard and it went across very well. It was a sell-out crowd. People came from M.I.T. and all the Boston colleges. And when it was over, Seymour Harris said he wanted to print it. So, we had it published in the *Review of Economics and Statistics* under the name of Gutt. I was accustomed to having papers written by me published under other names. I wrote three articles published at various times in *Foreign Affairs*, under three different names. I wrote a paper in the name of Harry White and another in the name of Secretary Vinson in 1946. Many years later I wrote a paper under the name of Leo Model, "The Politics of International Investment."

S.B.: Let me get back to the question about the parities. You actually tried to calculate for each country, what was the exchange rate that would help them recover their export markets.

Bernstein: That's right. Or, at least that wouldn't interfere with the recovery of their exports.

S.B.: But you were not, in some sense, trying to get them a competitive depreciation, were you?

Bernstein: No. We weren't really at that stage. Let me put it this way: Keynes, who had often talked about the problem of the postwar exchange rates, said to us (and I think quite properly), "Don't look at the prices we have in a period of scarcity; look at our costs. We've been very successful, and so have the Europeans," he said, "in keeping wages under control during the war." Well, I had already myself come to the conclusion that the main reason for controlling prices during the war was to keep wages from getting out of hand by responding to the rise in prices.

So, we had no reason for thinking that the cost level had gotten out of hand. If we were talking about anything that had changed, it was the real competitive position, in another sense. The United States now had built up an enormous new industrial structure, and it was ready to export everywhere. During the next few years, the Europeans would need to have an import surplus to supplement their own resources for reconstruction. And the role of the United States in world trade would be permanently greater than it had been before the war, and that affected the pattern of exchange rates. We knew all of that. But the main point was, we weren't trying to get a purchasing power parity based on prices. Nobody denied for a second that the Europeans were enormously successful in holding down costs.

There was another problem that was very important all through this period, and it came up at this same Harvard speech. I had already come to the conclusion that there would be several years of inflation after the war because of what I called latent inflation. During the war the public could not spend their incomes in the usual way because no consumer durable goods were produced and some nondurable goods were scarce. So people increased their savings, and private wealth became very large relative to present and prospective personal incomes. Because of this, the public had less need to save immediately after the war, particularly when automobiles and other durable goods became available again.

Besides, the wealth accumulated during the war was almost entirely in money-type assets--cash balances and government bonds. I said that after the war the public would want more of their wealth in real assets like houses and common stocks. Business firms too were unable to invest in plant and equipment and depleted their inventories during the war. They would want to use the reserves they held in cash and securities to buy real assets needed in production. The extra spending by consumers and business would raise prices, and the shift from money-type assets to real assets would result in a change in the prices of these assets--specifically, a fall in bond prices and a rise in stock prices and in prices for real estate. I published this in *Staff Papers*, the first article in the first issue.

Now, the Europeans--some of them--had themselves started to work on this problem. Belgium decided to freeze bank balances and release them gradually. At this time, when I made my first visit to the Netherlands, the new governor of the Bank of the Netherlands, Holtrop, said to me, "Professor Bernstein," (the Europeans used to call me 'Professor') "you know that we have been working in the Netherlands on this question. We were working on it during the German occupation. We met quietly, a number of the economists, and discussed the question, what's going to happen to the inflation when the Germans go out and we have all of this money." And they had some technical questions they put to me: How would you analyze this or that. It made them feel they had been on the right track because they had been working on the same problem.

When Gutt made this speech on initial par values at Harvard, the question came up about the inflation and how Belgium was dealing with it. Paul Samuelson asked him, "Well, how do you fit this into the concept that inflation is due to excessive demand?" Gutt turned the question over to me to answer. And the answer was that because of the wealth accumulated during the war, the personal savings rate will drop. People will spend more out of their current income until they've adjusted their wealth to what is proper for the income levels they're at. This was quite a meeting at Harvard, and it did much to create respect for the work of the Fund staff.

I have already said we were going to need new exchange rates when the first U.S. recession came. In the meantime I had been trying to persuade the British and others and my staff too, that we're going to need a change in the par values of the European currencies. And some of them were reluctant to face the fact that sterling would have to be devalued. I had on my staff a man named Maurice Allen who was an assistant director under me (later went to the Bank of England and became an Executive Director, and so on). He had been teaching at

Oxford and Lionel Robbins recommended him to me and he was really very good. There was only one thing wrong with him: he had a lot of class consciousness and he thought that somehow, because I was the director I should be called "Sir," even though he was older than I--or at least the same age. Well, I had to persuade my staff on what we had to do. So I did this in a little memorandum which was called, "The Marginal Incremental Rate of Exchange." I also gave this paper orally to the Washington Chapter of the Statistics Association.

The theme of this paper was the following: You have a country which has price controls. And you have an exchange rate which overvalues the currency in some sense. That means that you have a volume of imports which is excessively small, and you have to have rationing and price controls. Wouldn't the country be better off if it depreciated the currency, got the extra foreign exchange receipts from additional exports, let imports increase, but let the prices of imports rise in local currency? If the exchange rate for sterling were reduced from $4.00 to $2.80 a pound, the increment of receipts at the margin might be only $2.00 for the last pound of exports. But if the restriction on imports had been very severe, consumers and business firms would be better off to have a larger supply even if they paid 40 percent more for the imported goods. This was one of the papers that we used to convince countries that they would be better off if they devalued their currencies. Incidentally, Marcus Fleming used a similar analysis in his paper on the "Optimum Tariff" which he wrote without seeing or knowing of my paper on the marginal incremental rate of exchange.

Another problem came up in the Mexican depreciation. The Mexican peso was one of the currencies on my list for prospective devaluation. The Mexicans had a large inflation during the war. They were booming from our war, and they weren't doing much to restrain the expansion of the money supply and they had a big rise in prices and costs. Now the war was over, prices were going up, and the exchange rate couldn't be held, especially as the Mexicans had absolutely free capital flows. They came to the Fund for a change in the par value, and Jack Polak, who had just joined me, wrote a paper in which he explained that if the change in the par value was to have an effect on the trade balance and the current account, Mexico would have to reduce consumption and investment by the government or the private sector in order to free resources for export and to reduce the absorption of imports, although part of the improvement in the balance of payments could come from the increase in output induced by the devaluation.

When Sidney Alexander came to work for the Fund he went through all the papers we had written, and he decided that two of them would be worth doing something with. One of them was the paper on the marginal rate of exchange, and the other was Jack Polak's paper. He never did finish the one on the marginal incremental rate of exchange, but he used Polak's paper to develop the absorption theory of the effect of exchange depreciation on the trade balance. Later at a meeting at Princeton, Mr. Fritz Machlup wanted to know how this theory fits in with elasticities in the demand for imports and the supply of exports. I replied that the aggregate change in the trade balance depends upon the change in the absorption relative to the change in output. How that's distributed between an increase in exports and a decrease in imports, if there is one, depends on the relative elasticities. That's the role of the elasticities, to determine how much of the change in absorption--relative to output--will be in exports and imports.

Well, I put this, as well as a lot of the monetarism that was then dominating us, into a paper called, "Strategic Factors in Balance of Payments Adjustment." It starts with Adam Smith and earlier. If the Bank of England prints too much money, Smith said, it will not increase the money stock, as the excess will go abroad in the outflow of gold and silver.

Around 1948 my research staff was getting a wonderful reputation in Washington. And Alger Hiss came to see me. I knew Alger Hiss from the State Department. When I first met him he was in the Far Eastern division and it was in connection with what the Treasury did with the Japanese that I met him in the State Department. He always opened meetings of this kind by explaining what the State Department's objective was in dealing with the Japanese. The Treasury, as usual, was for stronger measures; it didn't mind what it did to the Japanese. And that's how I got to know Alger Hiss. I knew his brother much better, because his brother, Donny, was an assistant to Acheson, and Acheson usually spoke to me when he wanted the Treasury to do something because I was the one who was more likely to agree with him. Once he called and said, "Eddie, I'm talking to you as acting Secretary of the Treasury." Meaning that it was up to me to get the higher Treasury officials to agree to what the State Department wanted done.

Alger Hiss was then President of the Carnegie Endowment, having left the State Department. He was a favorite of John Foster Dulles, who didn't know about Hiss's views in the 1930s. I don't know why he should because it is probable that by then Alger Hiss had changed his mind about the Soviet Union and Communism. When Hiss called on me he asked me how we had such a good staff at the Fund, because everybody was talking about its quality. Most economists who had a choice between coming to us and other institutions chose us. I said, "We have a good one because first, we are very careful in our selection. Everyone gets an oral examination, we go over their records and look at the papers they've written. And we make the Fund a very attractive place to work by encouraging new ideas." And in fact, the Fund was very innovative in its thinking.

When the Marshall Plan came along, the U.S. Treasury took the view that there wasn't any need for credits from the Fund. I tried to get a concept across that the Dutch had brought to me. The Marshall Plan financed some of their imports from the United States, but it did not give them the money until some months after they had paid for the imports. At that time, the Europeans had not yet built up their cash balances. I tried to get the Fund into the business of offering "bridge finance"--that is, credits until they were reimbursed. The Treasury wasn't interested in that.

I'm going to cover one other exchange rate problem that came up, where we had to do some inventing, and then I'm going to come to the problem of the depreciation of the European currencies. The French wanted to depreciate the franc in 1948. They didn't want to depreciate it against sterling; they wanted to depreciate it against the dollar. Admittedly sterling was reaching the stage where it would need to be devalued.

What the French wanted to do was the following: They wanted to depreciate the franc by roughly twenty to twenty-five percent against the dollar and let the dollar rate float, but leave the rate for sterling unchanged. When I speak of sterling in this statement, it is as a surrogate for all the European currencies. There wasn't anything wrong with their devaluing the franc, but I was troubled about their having two rates: one for sterling and one for the dollar. When the French made this proposal, I met with Jack Polak and Bob Triffin, my most imaginative economists, and we talked this question out in front of the fireplace at my house until we understood what the problem was.

If the Fund approved the French proposal, we would have commodity arbitrage through the exchange market. French manufacturers could buy wool in Australia, at the sterling rate, do the processing, and then sell the woolen cloth in the United States at the dollar rate. They would make twenty or twenty-five percent on the wool content merely through the exchange rate. And we described this as "exchange arbitrage through commodities." I wrote the paper on this and it was signed by Triffin and me. I might say, I wrote so many papers then that I thought it would not look right to have them all in my name. We had a number of ways of disguising it. Some of my papers were issued as "a memorandum by the Research Department," or "a memorandum by Bernstein and someone else," who had worked with me on the subject. If the paper was written by someone else, even with help from me, it was issued in the name of the writer.

Well, the Fund turned down the French proposal and it also made France ineligible for drawing on the Fund.

S.B.: That must be one of the few cases of rejection of an exchange rate proposal.

Bernstein: There were very few. By the way, the U.S. Treasury was divided on the French proposal and they used that floating exchange rate rather than disparate cross rates as the reason for turning it down. In the view of the staff it was the disparate cross rates, not the floating rates, that mattered.

I wasn't getting along very well with the U.S. Treasury at this time. Mr. Snyder had called me in soon after he became Secretary of the Treasury to get my advice at the time of the first annual meeting. And I told him, "Mr. Secretary, I'm now an international civil servant. And you have Mr. White and his alternate as your representatives at the Fund. It's they who ought to be giving you advice." White resigned under pressure in 1948, and he died in 1949.

We'd had some devaluations prior to 1949, but they weren't significant. Nineteen forty-nine represented a big change. I described it at the time and justified it, as the readjustment of the international economic position of the rest of the world to the United States, as it had been affected by the Great Depression and the war. Now the question was, how do we go about changing the par values?

The first problem was to get them to see that they had to devalue the currency. By the way, recession had begun. This was the date when I said we'd have to change the par values. Early in 1949, the U.S. Executive Director began to press for discussions on the devaluation of the European currencies. I thought that a discussion by the Executive Directors would become public and result in speculation against the currencies before the Europeans were ready to devalue. The right way would have been for the Managing Director and me to visit the European members to discuss the exchange rate problem. The Bank of England said they did not want the Managing Director to come because it would lead to rumors of a devaluation of sterling.

So we had to start these visits without the Managing Director and without visiting the Bank of England. I went to the Netherlands with a few of the staff and during the discussion they said to me, "We understand very well that there has to be a change in the exchange rate. But don't ask us to do it first, because we're going to change our par value at the same time and to the same extent that the British change theirs." That is to say, they would not agree to changes in the intra-European exchange rates. That was also the attitude of the other countries, so that the first move would have to be made by the United Kingdom.

Well, I went to the Bank of England then. And the Bank of England accepted the visit. The Governor was Lord Cobbold. I had with me Maurice Allen, an assistant director of research. He had been a fellow of Balliol, one of the Oxford Colleges. The Governor of the Bank of England was Cobbold whom I had known since 1943; we went over the payments situation and the Governor said that it was really bad. And I said to him, "We have to remedy it. And don't forget that the best remedy is to devalue the currency." He said that he had it in mind, but he was not prepared to say when they will do it, or by how much sterling would be devalued. "Incidentally," he said to me, "it'll be for the Chancellor of the Exchequer to decide. No doubt he'll ask me, but nevertheless, he is the one that will have to do it."

I have been blamed for the fact that the Fund didn't make studies on the amount by which each currency should be devalued. The truth of the matter is that if we had made the studies, they would have been handed out automatically, to all of the directors. And word would have gone out that Bernstein was planning how much devaluation there shall be of sterling and each of the other currencies. So there was a big problem. It wasn't like initial Par Values, where we were going to say, "This is all right, with some qualifications." Besides our reports came out simultaneously with the approval of the initial par values. The Managing Director agreed with me that we should not have reports on changes in the par values which we would have to keep secret. And in any case, what could we have done if we had prepared such papers? We knew very well what the position of these countries was and we knew the attitude of the Netherlands that they were going to do exactly what the British did because they didn't want to disrupt the pattern of European rates that was working reasonably well in intra-European trade.

The British had a problem of their own. Their problem came in the following way: There was all this blocked sterling amounting to four billion pounds and it was leaking out in markets for blocked sterling that differed from country to country according to source. If anyone wanted to import from England, he could arrange with an Indian to get the sterling exchange and buy it from him at a discount in dollars. There were other markets with implicit rates for sterling, as in the sterling price of gold. So you could have said there were a half-dozen sterling rates for the dollar, either directly or implicitly--most of them directly. And the British had to decide which rate would minimize the leaks from the sterling balances. We could have told them what we thought would have been reasonable. In fact, we thought a rate of about three dollars would be reasonable.

S.B.: You told them that.

Bernstein: Well, we didn't tell them to propose that rate. But I told them my staff thought that about three dollars would seem reasonable for sterling. The British, however, decided to take what they thought was the lowest working rate, and that was $2.80. Now, the difference between $2.80 and $3.00 is around seven percent. At that time it would not have made much economic sense to say that a $3.00 rate would have been better than $2.80. Actually, the new rate had a very favorable effect on the free markets for sterling. Remarkably, the sterling price of gold fell after the devaluation. And I wrote a little note entitled, "The Devaluation of Sterling and the Sterling Price of Gold." What happened was that people had been uncertain how much devaluation there would be. So they quoted the sterling price of gold at what they thought the devaluation would be--that is, at less than $2.80 to the pound. But when the devaluation turned out to be a little bit less, the sterling price of gold dropped to reflect it.

You wanted to know if we ever had another case where we had a rejection of a proposed par value. The Germans and the Austrians were delayed members of the IMF. And I was sent out to Austria to find an exchange rate.

S.B.: When was that?

Bernstein: Oh, it was 1953. The way you get the exact date is to look in the IFS for when the first par value was declared to the Fund.

S.B.: I've seen it.

Bernstein: Well, they entertained me royally there. The President of the Austrian Bank was a man named Rizza, an Italian name. The Austrians have good economists and we had very good conversation on the Austrian situation.

S.B.: Did the Russians cause any trouble?

Bernstein: No. The Austrians took me through the Russian sector on a number of occasions. There was no trouble. I was with the Managing Director. The Austrians took us to the Abbey of Maelk. It is a very famous place. The Habsburgs had an apartment there and Napoleon captured the Abbey, which had been a fortress. In the technical discussions, I agreed with the Austrians on an initial par value.

S.B.: Now was this a new Austrian currency?

Bernstein: No, it was the schilling. I came back and wrote a memorandum on what we thought of the rate. I said it may seem a little high, but if the Austrians think they can hold it, they ought to be given a chance to do it. Well, the Treasury had become real tough. Everybody's going to toe the line and the bigger the devaluation the better. I took the view that we were going to push them into a bigger devaluation than was necessary, and I stood up for it in the Executive Board. What finally happened was that the Fund did not accept the proposed par value and the Austrians agreed to modify it slightly. It was a drastic step for the Executive Board not to accept a par value recommendation of the staff. Obviously, the Treasury had more power than I, and the Treasury opposed me.

S.B.: Why was that?

Bernstein: Well, the Treasury felt that first, I was too international. Even when the Treasury invited me to see them, as Mr. Snyder did, I advised him to ask his executive directors. We had trouble on what the Fund should do on the French rate. Frank Southard, who was then the director of monetary research at the Treasury, had asked to see me and I talked to him. He said, "Wouldn't you like to explain to my staff why you take this view?" I said, "No, Frank." I said, "My role has always been that I don't appeal to the staff against their director. You gave me a free chance to talk to you and I have had that." Frank Southard should have been very friendly with me, but he wasn't. We both came from an academic background. He had been a professor at Cornell. We had both been assistant directors of monetary research at the Treasury in 1941. Our careers separated when he went into the Navy and I left the Treasury for the Fund. We were never intimates, but we weren't rivals, and there was no animosity between us until 1948 when he became an executive director at the Fund. Until 1950 the Research Department comprised nearly all of the technical staff. There was a small operations department and a Treasurer's office, but the analytical work and the policy recommendations came from the Research Department. In 1950, led by the U.S. executive director, the Executive Board decided to create new departments out of the regional divisions of the Research Department. This was desirable as the number of members of the Fund increased. I did not like the creation of an Exchange Restrictions Department, particularly as it was to be headed by a division chief whom I had appointed to appease Harry White and whose ambition led him into what I regarded as conspiracies against me. His name was Irving Friedman and my wife had cautioned me against appointing him merely to please White. The reorganization still left the Research Department the largest and most influential department in the Fund.

And when this was done, the Managing Director, Gutt, wanted to show that he had confidence in me. So he proposed at the same time to raise my salary (which was very good even by those standards), and the U.S. Executive Director opposed it. The interesting thing was that he didn't get any support except from the Italians. The only ones who opposed the proposal to give me an increase in salary were the United States and Italy.

S.B.: So it went through?

Bernstein: Yes, it went through. Actually, the Treasury could seldom win a fight against me, if I stood up on a matter of principle. The most they could get was for me to compromise. But this was a terrible shock to them: That at the Fund, I had more influence with the Europeans and even with the developing countries (there weren't many developing countries) than the Treasury. Most of the issues were on policies and procedures. The Fund was selling almost no exchange to its members in 1950-55.

S.B.: It wasn't doing much on the operations side.

Bernstein: That's right. And the reason was that a policy was adopted by the Fund which said, so long as there were the enormous sums available through the Marshall Plan there wouldn't be any transactions. This would not apply to the developing countries but they were well supplied with reserves. Some of them used the reserves very foolishly. Argentina, for example, bought back its railroads from the British to get rid of its sterling balances. And these railroads were losing money, and of course, under the Argentines they lost three times as much! The British were very wise in selling some investments for sterling. They sold off the Indian railroads and they sold off the pension claims of Britain against India. The British took over the obligation to provide pensions for British nationals in the Indian Civil Service.

So we are back to the point that the Fund was not engaging in exchange transactions with the Europeans at this time. Actually, their payments position had begun to improve rapidly.

The Europeans were adding a billion dollars a year to their reserves--half of it in gold and half in dollars. The gold was the newly mined production and sales of the Soviet Union that was not absorbed in private hoards and in the arts and industry. U.S. gold reserves were sightly larger at the end of 1957 than they had been at the end of 1950, although less than at their peak in early 1949. The depletion of U.S. gold reserves came later and it was a problem that I dealt with after I resigned from the Fund.

In 1950 we began to make more of the technical work of the fund available to the public. We started *International Financial Statistics* which was directed by Earl Hicks, who had been the assistant in my money course at Chapel Hill. Allan G.B. Fisher, the distinguished New Zealand economist, was one of the research chiefs and he urged me to follow the advice of Dennis Robertson, who said it was a shame that some of the Fund's papers didn't get into the public domain. And so we started *Staff Papers* with Fisher as editor. So we had two publications, with Earl Hicks in charge of one and Allan Fisher editing the other. And by then we were at the end of Mr. Gutt's term as managing director.

Because of the opposition of the United States, his contract was not renewed when it expired.

S.B.: When was that?

Bernstein: Well, it expired in 1951, five years after '46. And we got a nonentity, Rooth, a former governor of the Bank of Sweden. I got along very well with him but he was a cautious person, not one to stand up to the United States. He disappeared after five years and we got Per Jacobsson. He came in at a time when the Fund was in a good position to resume work.

S.B.: Were you still not making many transactions?

Bernstein: Until then very little. In 1956, the Fund was ready to resume operations with Europe. The Marshall Plan had stopped. The European countries were under pressure because of the Suez incident. As you know, the Suez incident resulted in an enormous increase in U.S. reserves in '56, '57, a bad blow to Europe. And also by now, the developing countries had used up most of their reserves and they were in need of help from the Fund. It was a good time to get started again.

S.B.: And there was a U.S. recession in '57 also.

Bernstein: And there was a U.S. recession in 1957-58 and that was important for the developing countries. For Europe, '58 was strangely a good year in the balance of payments. World trade dropped in '58. But the European position improved because they had the Suez open again. We can see all this in the reserve position of the United States, and also in the U.S. trade position. Nineteen fifty-eight would normally have been a good year for the U.S. balance of payments, but it was actually a bad year. From the end of 1957 until the end of 1958 U.S. gold reserves dropped by 65 million ounces--$2.3 billion. There wasn't much change in our other reserves. External liabilities to foreign central banks went up about a billion dollars. But the big drop was in our gold and I will discuss that later.

So this was a good time to resume operations. I didn't get along with Jacobsson. There were all sorts of reasons for this. Some of it may have been that Jacobsson was a bit jealous and he may have been resentful because I hadn't been very friendly to the BIS during the war. In fact I had a run-in with the president of the BIS, an American.

S.B.: Jacobsson came from the BIS.

Bernstein: He was the economic advisor to the BIS, and had a tremendous reputation with the New York bankers who didn't really know much about economics. We started out in a very friendly way. When he came to the Fund we had a big dinner for him, and after the dinner he took me aside and said to me, "I'm going to make an inaugural speech tomorrow." In the speech he wanted to say that all the developing countries ought to reorganize their banking systems so that they'd be like that of the United States, or the United Kingdom (he was a great Anglophile). And what did I think of that as an inaugural speech. Well, I said to him, "The general idea's all right. But you can't ask countries to change the structure of their banking system, because these are institutional growths that come out of long histories, and to ask them to change that is really impractical. But whatever the institutional arrangements of their banking systems, there's no reason why they shouldn't have the same conservative credit policies and monetary policies as the United States and the United Kingdom." And that is what he said in his inaugural speech to the Directors.

Jacobsson had a parochial outlook. The Managing Director had to make periodic visits to members of the Fund. Once, after returning from a visit to Latin America, Jacobsson told the Executive Directors that he was surprised to find these countries so advanced. Apparently, he thought all civilization was confined to Europe with an offshoot in the United States and Canada. He thought he would find Latin America backward and was astonished that the ministers and governors in these countries were educated and aware of their problems. The Executive Directors laughed at him when he made that report to them.

I used to have breakfast with him frequently (he wanted to have breakfast with me) and I would explain what we were doing in the Research Department and what we'd have to do. He kept asking me about Keynes; he didn't know Keynes well. Once he asked me whether I thought he was as good an economist as Keynes. I brushed the question off gently. To say anything like that would be complete nonsense because he wasn't much of an economist.

Once after he had come back from a trip to Europe, I had just been there but without him, and I had come back with a strong view that we would have trouble with the franc and with sterling, though maybe their par values could survive. This was right after Suez. When Jacobsson came back, he made a speech to the senior staff in which he said that he was convinced all the exchange rates were right. And the evidence that they're right is that wage rates were exactly the same in all of the large European countries. (I suppose he meant excluding Italy.) And then he turned to me, looking for confirmation, and he said, "Isn't that so, Eddie?" I said, "Mr. Chairman, I don't think the wages are exactly the same in all of these countries. But if they were, I would regard that as evidence that the exchange rates are unlikely to be right, because I can't believe that they are all equally productive." Well, he swallowed that. The staff might have been a bit surprised but they were accustomed to my saying frankly exactly what I thought.

Soon after Jacobsson became Managing Director, I told him we were committed to making two reports. The first was the consequence of a meeting in 1956 of the Governors of the Central Banks of Europe, the United States and Canada. At this meeting, Maurice Frere, the former Governor of the National Bank of Belgium and then President of the BIS, wanted the Fund to establish regulations that would require the members of the IMF who drew on the Fund to deposit with the Fund actual currency or a deposit at the central bank instead of giving it non-interest bearing notes of the government. What he was after had merit.

In 1947, the Belgians, who came out of the war best of all the occupied countries, came to the Fund to borrow 20 million dollars, or some such figure. I had to write a note on this at that time. So my first answer to the managing director, Gutt, was that the Belgians wouldn't possibly need dollars. They are the ones with the best payments position in Europe today. So why don't we ask them what payments they have to make that require them to get 20 million dollars from the Fund. It turned out that the government wanted the 20 million dollars, because then it would sell the exchange to the central bank and get Belgian francs for it. The central bank was not allowed to lend the government the money, but it could buy the exchange from them with Belgian francs. The Fund had to tell Belgium that it could not draw on the Fund for that purpose.

Frere had been the governor at that time. Now, eight or nine years later, he wanted to make sure that governments could not finance the budget deficit with the local currency counterpart of foreign exchange drawn from the Fund. He wanted the counterpart deposited with the central bank to the credit of the Fund. Thus, the liability of the central bank for the local currency would be to the Fund. The consequence of such a rule would have been that the government couldn't have got the local currency equivalent for its own use.

S.B.: This would even be a reserve tranche or a gold tranche borrowing, at that time.

Bernstein: Yes, it wouldn't have made any difference. Whatever they drew, they would have to put the local currency on deposit in the name of the Fund. The governors discussed it at the meeting, after the luncheon, and then they agreed to have me write a memorandum on it. So I had an instruction from the 1956 meeting of the governors.

There was another report to which we were committed. In 1956, a man named Callaghan, who was the executive director for Australia and for South Africa, came to me and asked me whether I would be willing to have the Research Department make a study on the adequacy of reserves. I said to him, "We haven't made such a study in several years. It's time we made another one." And so we had that on the board when Rooth went out. I told that to Mr. Jacobsson when he became managing director.

On the first question on the local currency counterpart, I wrote a memorandum in which I said that there was no sense in requiring the deposit of local currency. What we really want, and what's really important for the Fund, is that when a country draws on the Fund, we want to make sure it doesn't become the basis for an expansion of credit. The Fund should make sure that countries that say they need to draw on the Fund and do draw on the Fund don't hold the funds as foreign exchange reserves and then use them for an expansion. As usual, the emphasis in my memorandum was on policy, not mechanics.

Mr. Jacobsson didn't like the memorandum. He didn't like it because he wanted to do what Frere wanted. After all, Frere was then the president of the BIS. He had scribbled along the sides of my paper some notes in which he differed with it. So I said to him, "Mr. Chairman, I'll be glad to rewrite this memorandum to say exactly what you wish. But then we'll have to tell these people at the luncheon when we meet them in 1957, that this is a paper that represents the views of the Managing Director. And if they ask why I didn't write the paper, we would explain that any paper submitted to them had to reflect the views of the Fund rather than of an individual." Jacobsson said he didn't want to do it that way; he would go along with what I've written. The paper got an enormous reception from the governors and they asked to have it printed in *Staff Papers*. Well, Mr. Jacobsson basked in this, as if he had done it. He was glad to have the credit, especially as Mr. Southard in his speech pointedly gave him the credit although he knew I wrote the paper. That didn't bother me; I was accustomed to this. The report was printed, although without my name.

We now had to do the report on reserves, a much more difficult problem. After I explained the need to write the report, Jacobsson asked me to bring up the staff that was going to work on the reserves. I brought up Jack Polak, who was my deputy, I brought up Goode, Altman, and one or two others. And so four or five of us came to see the Managing Director. I gave him the history of the request, and explained how we would have to do it statistically and analytically. At that point Jacobsson said that in his view it didn't matter how much reserves there were. We could get along with any level of reserves, provided wages and prices were fitted to it. I said that it is very hard to fit the level of wages and prices to reserves if they grow too slowly. It would be better to provide for a growth of reserves that would be consistent with the growth of the world economy. After some discussion Jacobsson said, "I'd like this study to be made under my direction." So, I said to him, "These men are going to do the work under your supervision, and they will report directly to you. And if there's anything that they're doing that you think ought to be done differently and you think I could help that way, all you have to do is let me know." So, I turned the supervision of the report over to him.

I not only turned it over to him, but I made plans to quit the Fund. So, I accepted an invitation from Harvard to teach at the summer school there in '57. The study was going on without me. I had told Jack Polak to take charge of the staff, as I had told the Managing Director I would not be in charge; I did want the study to be a good one.

And that is the story of my relations with Mr. Jacobsson, the Managing Director. Soon after I returned from my summer teaching, I went to see the deputy managing director and I told him I would resign. I didn't go to see Jacobsson at all. I wrote a letter of resignation, intending to leave the Fund on December 31st, which would have been a convenient bookkeeping date for me and for the Fund. Actually I didn't leave until January 8, 1958. I had commitments to make speeches--commitments for the Fund--and I felt I had to fill them. The people to whom I spoke would have been shocked to know that I had resigned from the Fund. The extra week made it possible for me to fill my engagements without any interruption.

S.B.: Can we go back to one point on the Fund before we go on to this issue, and that is this: It sounds to me as though the paper concerning the question of the deposit of currency and your suggestions on that were part of the policy that relates to the question of conditionality, as it's now understood, in that general vein. The question of how the country is going to use funds that it was obtaining from the IMF, whether it was going to repay them, whether it had a program of . . .

Bernstein: Well, we didn't have any question of repayment. In the report on counterpart funds we emphasized that what was important was policy, not the mechanics of the transaction with the Fund. Under conditionality, we have a formal commitment by the country to follow an agreed program, usually in the form of a letter from the minister of finance. In those days, what we used to do on a drawing was simply to talk to the country's officials, write a little memorandum on what needs to be done, the country would say it intended to do all this, and that would be it.

The suggestion of Frere dealt with a different concept. By the way, the British and the Americans both were utterly opposed to the notion that they would have to put up money as a deposit in a central bank when and if they drew on the Fund; so they were right behind me on this issue. No, this was really not a question of what policies a country would follow, but whether it should get local currency finance as a by-product of a drawing on the Fund. Ordinarily, when the government borrows money abroad and sells the foreign exchange to the Central Bank, the money supply would be increased. The public might then buy the exchange and the money supply would then be decreased. And you would have made no ultimate change in the money supply, although the government's balances would go up and the public's would go down until the government spent the money and the public's balances were replenished. The Frere proposal was that the government should not be able to treat drawings on the Fund as if they were loans to finance its budget. For a government that had difficulty in borrowing in the market, the Frere proposal would compel it to follow a more cautious fiscal policy. For governments, like those of the United Kingdom and the United States, with easy access to the market, the Frere proposal would have had no effect on policy and would have added nominally to its interest expenditures shown in the budget, although obviously having no net effect. So it was a technique to deprive governments of easy financing that Frere had in mind. It really had no great significance on any question except the one that worried him: that the government of Belgium would use this device to get money to finance itself.

S.B.: Right. I see the point.

Bernstein: And we were quite sure we could stop that without the Frere proposal.

S.B.: Now, on the same question. Can you recall when--I think it was the case at some point during the '50s--the Fund did begin to require countries (even on an informal basis by some means of understanding) to enter into some kinds of engagements as to what they would do.

Bernstein: There were several developments that occurred that I'm going to mention, including one in which I opposed a U.S. Treasury proposal. Just before the Fund started lending money once more, the Treasury proposed that every country that borrows from the fund should file a statement that it would repay the money within three years with an outside limit of five. Well, I didn't think that was unreasonable as a policy, but I didn't think we could do it legally by a requirement of this sort. As I thought it was a good policy, I suggested a legal way of doing it.

What I proposed was this: The Articles of Agreement said that when the charges on a country's net indebtedness to the Fund reached 4 percent on any of its drawings, the member must consult with the Fund on reducing its debt. Remember, we had a dual system of graduating the interest rates on drawings. The rate rose as a country borrowed in each higher bracket--that is, in tranches of 25 percent of its quota--and the rate rose further for each half year in which the debt was outstanding. In the table of charges adopted at Bretton Woods, it would have taken seven years to get to 4 percent on drawings in the first tranche--25 percent of the quota. The schedule of charges could be changed only by a three-fourths vote, to make sure that the Fund's interest rates would remain low. At Bretton Woods, Dennis Robertson said to me that with this requirement, the schedule of charges would never be changed. But actually, once the United States threatened to require a written commitment to repay at a fixed date, attitudes in the Fund changed. So I brought in a new table of charges under which, after 3 years, the interest rate on the first drawing reached 4 percent.

When I presented this to the board, the U.S. director said that it hadn't occurred to the Treasury that this was a way of doing what they wanted, but now that we had proposed it, they would like to have both--the commitment to repay in three to five years and the new schedule of charges. The Fund did adopt both. But now, when a country said it would repay the Fund in three to five years, it was taking cognizance of the fact that this was exactly what the table of charges required them to do. This was one of several disagreements I had with the U.S. Treasury.

When I resigned, the Fund got a large number of complaints from Europe, asking why it had let me go. And the managing director (this is Jacobsson), said that I had come to tell him that I was tired after 11 years on the same job, that it was time to change, and so on and so forth. Actually, there was no truth in this; I hadn't even gone to see him. I just handed him my resignation in writing.

The Fund held a large farewell reception, the staff of the Research Department elected me an honorary life-time critic and gave me a diploma, which I have kept. That was because I paid a great deal of attention to its publications, particularly *International Financial Statistics*. A few months later, at a dinner in Marcus Fleming's home, they asked me to come back to the Fund as Deputy Managing Director.

S.B.: They asked you. Who?

Bernstein: Those who were at the dinner--Jack Polak, head of research, Joe Gold, general counsel, and others. The dinner was organized for the purpose of getting me back. This was because of the pressure of members on Jacobsson. I learned about this pressure from his daughter who was writing his biography. She had to find the reason why I left the Fund. She told me what her father had written in his diary and the complaints he had had about letting me resign. He wanted me to return. I had had other indications of this. At the Fleming dinner the invitation was direct, "Would I be willing to come back to the Fund as Deputy Managing Director?" I said, "I'm doing fine where I am." "Oh," they said, "salary is no problem and you can have all the expenses you need." I suppose it would have been the equivalent to around 75 to 80 thousand dollars a year. But actually I was making more than that at EMB, Ltd. Just the same, I would have come back if it hadn't been for Jacobsson, because I had a strong institutional feeling for the Fund. But I said no.

5

EMB, Ltd.

Bernstein: At the time I resigned, I was not short of money, but I didn't have another job. I could have got a job teaching easily enough, but my wife didn't want that. During the summer session at Harvard, they all gave us a big party with the professors at M.I.T. and Harvard all saying how glad they are that I'd come. But she didn't enjoy it. In fact, she had to have an appendectomy while she was there at Massachusetts General Hospital. In the course of the next few years I had four or five offers from universities, but I decided not to go back to teaching. Actually, better opportunities came to me rather quickly.

After I left the Fund, I got letters from a number of Central Banks saying that they were going to miss the papers that I used to write. I thought about that and I replied that if they were going to miss my papers, I'd be glad to continue to write them and offer them on a subscription basis. I didn't know then how I would run the sub-scription service, but I was willing to try. I started by giving subscribers one paper a month that was reasonably long--nine or ten pages--and a shorter paper that was more topical. By the end of the year, I had developed a format that I continued for 23 years. That was to issue two research reports a month plus a letter on U.S. economic news every week or two weeks.

I started EMB, Ltd. early in 1958 and I made a lot of money out of it because I had nearly every central bank in Europe as subscribers, the BIS, the European Economic Community, Canada and Japan, and a number of developing countries. Southard kept the IMF from subscribing until he retired, at which time the Fund subscribed.

At first, I had great difficulty in finding the right way to run EMB, Ltd. I started by getting a group of people I knew, who had worked with me elsewhere. I had somebody who had been at the Treasury, Jack DeBeers; I had somebody who had been with me at the Fund to do Latin American work, named Felipe Pazos, who later became the

President of the Banco Nationale of Cuba (the central bank). He'd been at odds with most administrations in Cuba at one time or another--he had to escape, after Batista came in, and later from Castro. And, I'm afraid, I was one of those who persuaded him to go back when Castro first came in. In fact, for a while, I was an advisor to the Cuban National Bank down there. Then Haberler gave me a young man, who'd just gotten a Ph.D. from Harvard, and I put him on my staff.

I found very soon that to get a paper written by these people was very expensive. They needed three or four months to write a paper, because we had to cover a variety of subjects and they needed to research each paper from the ground up. It was costing my firm four and five thousand dollars a paper. Well, you can figure how expensive in-house research can be. What does it cost the government to get a good research report written, if a man works two or three months on it at three or four thousand dollars a month; that adds up to a lot of money. Besides which, in the case of the young man with the Harvard Ph.D., I had to rewrite his papers. He never seemed to know that he'd reached a conclusion. He really couldn't emphasize what was important. So, I used to have to rewrite them. Of course, after he'd done all the work, the rewriting was easy.

After a few years, I found that the easiest way to do our research reports was to have one full time assistant, four or five regular contributors, and a few others who wrote papers from time to time. They were all experts in their fields so that writing a paper for us did not require extended research. In the United States, about a half dozen professors wrote occasional papers in the EMB series. Our first regular contributor abroad was Frank Paish of the London School of Economics. He had worked with me at the Fund and he was excellent for our two reports a year on Britain.

When Paish retired, I had a problem in picking a successor because several people at the London School of Economics wanted the job. They asked their friends to write to me. Harry Johnson had a candidate of his own. In the end I picked Alan Day because Paish recommended him. I also had regular contributors in Canada, France, Switzerland, and Germany, and an occasional one in Mexico. In Germany, my contributor was a professor who had been the secretary of the Council of Economic Advisors. In Canada and in France, I used academic people who had been on my staff at the International Monetary Fund.

I chose people who were already thoroughly familiar with what they were going to do. They were writing on the subjects. All they had to do was bring the statistics up to date and they would give me a paper in a month. And as I paid them three thousand dollars for the paper, they were very pleased. Alan Day said to me, "You're very generous."

But EMB, Ltd. was doing so well, it didn't matter much to me one way or the other. So that's the way I ran EMB, Ltd.

S.B.: It's a very clever idea. I think it worked.

Bernstein: It worked very well.

S.B.: Because it combined the best ideas from all around. Don't rely entirely on your own . . .

Bernstein: I couldn't. Of course, I did a little editing, usually to shorten the papers but sometimes to point up the conclusions and sometimes to tone them down.

S.B.: So, if you look at the entire list of the EMB papers . . .

Bernstein: Half of them aren't mine. But you'll know which are mine when you read them. In the case of a French paper, for example, when Mitterand was elected, my correspondent wanted to have a very downhill paper--it was not going to be a good time for France. I didn't want to end the paper that way, and though he said all he wanted on it, we wound up the paper with the sentence that "In the end, what will determine what happens in France, is whether the pragmatism of Mitterand can overcome the dogmatism of the Socialist party." We did get all the criticism in, but we gave the paper an upbeat note.

S.B.: You gave him a little bit of hope.

Bernstein: That's right. We gave it an upbeat note, not because France was a subscriber but because the paper would have more influence that way.

The methods by which I used to get my thoughts across were primarily two. The first one was to write a paper issued as one of our research reports. It went to almost all the central banks. And then my job was to get the Treasury to accept my suggestion. When Kennedy was elected, that became easier, because I was among a large group of academic people who were brought in to consult with the Treasury and used to meet regularly. I gave a talk at almost every one of the sessions, usually a talk on the balance of payments or monetary reserves. Sometimes I gave a talk on the output effects (that's the cyclical effects) of the changes in our balance of payments, where the balance of payments was treated as a cause rather than a consequence of the rest of the economy.

Well, the Fund's report on the reserves came out in 1958, and I gave a talk at Harvard on that, entitled, "International Monetary Reserves." It was a seminar that got enormous publicity in official circles. Remember, this was a period when I was getting my subscribers. It helped me get subscribers. This paper took up the question of how reserves had grown so far and then it went on to say that the method of providing reserves which we had had up to then could not continue.

S.B.: The primary method was newly mined gold plus dollars from the U.S. balance of payments.

Bernstein: Until 1957. But beginning in 1958, they began to take gold from us on an enormous scale. Well, there is a statement in this paper in which I said, "This method of providing reserves cannot continue." I made several suggestions. The most important, the one that had practical effect, was the proposal for the Fund to enter into an agreement with its principal members under which they commit themselves to lend stated amounts to the Fund when needed to deal with serious payments difficulties. That was the origin of the Group of Ten and the General Arrangements to Borrow. Later the Joint Economic Committee asked me to write a report on the International Effects of U.S. Economic Policy.

And in this study for the government--Study Paper No. 16, it's called--I proposed it again. At that time Triffin was proposing a world central bank that would create reserves by lending money, while I proposed the G.A.B. so the Fund could borrow the money for extending reserve credit. The two proposals were rival methods of dealing with the reserve problem. It got a big play in the London *Economist*. Finally, the Treasury took it up, and the Fund adopted it.

Otto Eckstein was in charge of the JEC studies--they were part of a larger study of inflation--and in early 1960 he went to Europe. After he came back he told me that the central banks wanted to know the status of the Bernstein proposal. I got a lot of attention but no action until Douglas Dillon became secretary of the Treasury in 1961. The Treasury had a group of advisors, mainly professors, with Seymour Harris in charge, and they met with the Treasury officials and others from the Federal Reserve and the Council of Economic Advisors to discuss various problems, including the international monetary system. I tried to persuade the Treasury to back my proposal, and Dillon did.

S.B.: And this was adopted in . . .

Bernstein: 1961. I proposed it in October, 1958; proposed it again in December, 1959 in Study Paper No. 16, the Fund approved it in 1961, and it came into effect in 1962.

After Kennedy was elected, around December 27 or so, the *Wall Street Journal* said, "Bernstein is going to be Undersecretary for Monetary Affairs." I was giving a speech in New York the day that appeared. I had an overflow crowd. I had stopped in at the Federal Reserve Bank that morning and I got a very warm reception. As a practical matter, I couldn't be appointed. I think the mere association with White killed any possibility.

Well, this went on for several years. I told you that during this period the Fund asked me to come back--at least that's the way I interpreted it. My own feeling was that I was having a lot of fun and being very useful with my work. My series of papers was commenting on monetary policy and the balance of payments, and making all sorts of suggestions. I had come to the conclusion, by 1963, that we aren't going to be able to continue the provision of reserves in the same way as in the past. Of course, I knew that already in 1958. I had a paragraph in the paper on the reserve problem, in which I said we couldn't continue that method of reserves. Nevertheless, it was a tolerable method of reserves up to 1957. It was only in 1958 that Europe began to draw heavily on our gold reserves.

By 1963, the drain of gold from our reserves had become enormous. In the preceding five years, U.S. gold reserves fell by one-third, and more than half of the increase of Europe's reserves was in the form of gold, with the rest mainly in official holdings of dollars. I felt that we were running into a problem which I had defined differently, but essentially was what others were saying--primarily Bob Triffin, but also Milton Gilbert and Roy Harrod. I'm going to give you my analysis of Triffin's views a little later.

What troubled me was that we could no longer have equal attractiveness of the different reserve assets. I wrote a memorandum for the Dillon Committee on this question. We could no longer make the dollar equally attractive with gold merely through the interest rate. Higher interest rates would have an adverse effect on the economy; it wouldn't of itself be enough to reassure many of those countries that wanted gold instead of dollars. My second proposition was that if we were going to have the equal attractiveness of the reserve assets, we must get another reserve asset which would share with the dollar the burden of providing reserves so that we wouldn't expose the dollar to competition only with gold. The ultimate solution I suggested was to have countries put all of their different reserves--gold, dollars and a new reserve asset--in a Reserve Settlement Account. Countries would draw on their balances in this Account for balance of payments settlements.

Now, on the problem of equal attractiveness of reserves and the creation of a reserve asset . . . When Fred Deming came to the Treasury to replace Roosa as Undersecretary of the Treasury, Dillon said to him, "The first thing you have to do is to look into Bernstein's proposal for a reserve unit." In 1965, after Dillon resigned, the new Secretary, Fowler, appointed a committee under Dillon to advise the Treasury on what new arrangements it should propose on reserves. I had been advocating the creation of a Reserve Unit by the Group of Ten to be used along with gold in international settlements. There were several other proposals for dealing with the reserve question at that time. Bob Triffin was for establishing a world central bank. Roosa wanted to have a series of swaps among the large industrial countries and such arrangements had been made providing for such credits to be drawn as needed and repaid in a short period--typically six months. I argued that if we created a Reserve Unit which would be allocated among the Group of Ten and accepted by them as a reserve asset, we could in effect have activated and multilateralized the swap arrangements. Instead of having to draw on credit lines that would be repaid in a short period, the Group of Ten would issue 10 billion dollars of Reserve Units which would be used along with gold as final reserve assets. As I conceived it, with gold and Reserve Units the dependence on dollars for the growth of reserves would be very limited.

It seemed to me that the Reserve Unit had some advantages over the swaps which Roosa had arranged, although the same countries would be involved. With the Reserve Unit, a country wouldn't have to wait until it needed the reserves, which could be in a crisis. It would have the reserves on hand and using the Reserve Units wouldn't look like dealing with a crisis situation as drawing on the swap lines would.

Well, Roosa did come around to that in 1965 or so. He gave the Root lectures at the Council on Foreign Relations in New York which were published as a book. He proposed a loose form of the Reserve Unit. I didn't think much of his plan. The biggest trouble with his plan was the following: Under the Roosa Plan no country was obligated to accept the Reserve Units--that is, to hold more Reserve Units than were allotted to it. Well, you can't tell a group of countries, "Look, here are Reserve Units which are as good as gold" and then fail to provide assurance that they can be used in international settlements. Following a general rule which I did with every proposal for monetary reform, I wrote a memorandum in which I said what would have to be done to make the Roosa Plan work. "What you have to do," I said, "is to have at least a three-fold holding obligation. That is to say, if Germany has an allocation of five hundred million Reserve Units, it'll have to accept Reserve Units until it holds a billion and a half." Now, this would be making the plan at least twice as liquid as the general account of the IMF, where members, in effect, had to extend credit up to 100 percent of their quotas. Here, by holding 300 percent of their allocation, they would be extending twice as much credit as their allocation.

Roosa came to accept that fairly quickly. While we were in the midst of the discussion at the Dillon Committee, he and I were on a program of the Conference of Business Economists. After he explained his views and I explained mine--we were keeping it very low key--someone in the audience asked: "If you're going to create these reserves, don't you have to give countries the assurance that in fact they can be used? So, mustn't there be someone who has to take it?" I don't know who it was. By the way, Young was presiding at this meeting. He'd arranged the meeting. You know the Young I mean? From the Federal Reserve. And I think this persuaded Bob that it was necessary to have such a provision. And when the Group of Ten came around to writing the plan for creating a reserve asset, that was the provision that was put into the SDR arrangements. The term was used because of French opposition to having a Reserve Unit. But, they were willing to have Special Drawing Rights. And so, the easiest solution was to say, "We'll have a Reserve Unit and we'll call it Special Drawing Rights."

S.B.: You wanted to get back to Triffin and to Deming.

Bernstein: Deming was the one who told me that Dillon asked him to carry all this through. And of course, in all of this, Deming was the U.S. negotiator with the Group of Ten and IMF. He was very much in favor of the proposal I made, and he was extremely pleased that Bob Roosa and I got around to agreeing on a plan the Treasury would support.

I have to take Bob Roosa's views and show where they differed from mine. A memorandum on that is in my papers. One of the differences was the method of determining the allocation of Reserve Units. The British would have been allocated very little under the Roosa proposal. I thought his allocation formula was arbitrary. I said, we can distribute the Reserve Units or SDRs according to quotas, or some such formula. That made it much easier. The British were then very much in favor of my proposal but they certainly didn't like the original Roosa proposal.

By the way, when this was going on, the London *Economist* published a statement saying that Bernstein had opposed the Roosa plan in the meeting of the Treasury Committee on the reform of the international monetary system, by saying it was deflationary. Actually, I had never said that at all. What I said was that it wouldn't work because there was no accepting requirement. But I didn't feel that I could answer the London *Economist* about what I said at a Treasury meeting. They were quoting someone and happened to get it wrong. So I let it go; I didn't pay any attention to it. Their choice of the word "deflationary" came back to the little debate we had on the Triffin Plan.

Triffin proposed a plan to set up a central bank which would be empowered to lend reserves. Countries would deposit their gold and other assets and have a balance with the Central Bank. That didn't trouble me at all--that part. What troubled me was two other things. The first one was that the United States and the United Kingdom would retire the dollar and sterling deposits that other countries made. Well, these were enormous sums for that time. So I said, "For the United States to build up a surplus on an official reserve basis in order to retire the outstanding dollar reserves, in addition to financing foreign loans and direct investment abroad would be deflationary. The rest of the world, the Europeans especially, would not be able to accept such an increase in the U.S. surplus on current account. If you add to that the increase in the British surplus that would have been necessary to retire the sterling balances, the pressure on other industrial countries would have been deflationary, particularly as the increase in the current account surplus could not be invested abroad."

Well, Bob Triffin told me (he was then in Europe) that until I made that point, everybody had said that the Triffin Plan was inflationary. But when my criticism came out, they said it was deflationary. I'm not sure they all understood it, but the concept was, the Triffin Plan would be deflationary because the United States and Britain would have to run such large surpluses, that other countries would have to run large current account deficits which would contract their economy.

The other thing I objected to very much, was the notion that a central bank could operate by lending. As I pointed out in a letter--either to Triffin or the London *Economist*--in the United States, we've given up the notion that we can provide the reserves the banking system needs by discounts. What we do is to have open market operations. You would need a huge turnover of new borrowers, away from one group to a new group, to generate the increase in outstanding credits needed for a growth in aggregate reserves. It would be much better, I said, if we created the reserves through something equivalent to open market operations. We wouldn't have to wait for countries to come and borrow, we would create the reserves they would need. And of course, that's what we do. The method we use now, the allocation of SDRs, is the equivalent of open market operations. Drawings on the General Account of the IMF are, so to speak, discount operations. Allocations of SDRs are really open market operations. The initiative is taken by the Fund; it doesn't have anything to do with any one country needing reserve credit.

S.B.: The Fund creates the reserves with which it buys assets from its members, essentially when they need the reserves.

Bernstein: In the General Account, the part of the Fund created at Bretton Woods, the Fund lends foreign exchange to a member based on its quota or a waiver of its quota. In return, it receives a non-interest bearing note of the country, although it levies a transactions charge and if the credit is outstanding for more than a short period it also collects a continuous use charge--interest. In the Special Account, the Fund creates SDRs and allocates them to members. What the Fund has as the counterpart is a claim against the member on its books. When a member runs down the SDRs allocated to it, it pays the Fund interest on its net use of the SDRs. The Fund, in turn, pays members who have accumulated SDRs interest on the amount they hold in excess of their allocation. The allocation of SDRs is like open market operations in the sense that they are reserves supplied on the initiative of the Fund.

S.B.: So, the obligation that the country undertakes, if I understand correctly--it has two obligations: It undertakes to supply its own or another transferable currency against SDRs, when they're used; or it undertakes to accept SDRs. Well, that's the same thing.

Bernstein: In addition, it pays interest on any SDRs it uses. So, it is, in effect, like an open market operation. It doesn't have to ask for credit. It already has the reserves and the interest it pays is very low.

S.B.: Well, not now. It's been increased, of course.

Bernstein: Even so, it's not the rate of interest which these countries would have to pay if they were borrowing dollars in the market.

The other idea that I had proposed was what later came to be called the Substitution Account. That was the consolidation of all the reserve assets in a single Reserve Settlements Account. The reserves would not be deposited in these accounts; they would be earmarked. The member would get a credit balance denominated in Composite Reserve Units.

S.B.: When was this proposed?

Bernstein: About 1967. In one form or another even earlier. But, in the form I'm giving to you now, 1967. And there's a whole file of materials explaining why and how; what its logic was and so forth.

S.B.: Was this in an EMB, Ltd. paper?

Bernstein: Yes. All of these proposals were in EMB, Ltd. papers. All of them. It was because of the importance of these ideas that some central banks subscribed to my papers.

S.B.: Because I knew the substitution account came up later in the C-20 negotiations.

Bernstein: I didn't use this term. Later it was said, "Well, after all, you proposed the substitution account. Why aren't you in favor of it now?" In fact, I'd proposed it in different forms several times. Let me get the first proposal. Every country would earmark in the Reserve Settlement Account its gold, its dollars, and other eligible foreign exchange. It then gets a credit in Composite Reserve Units (CRUs). A country can't use these reserves separately. It can keep working balances in dollars, but it can't keep additional reserves in dollars. That means, if a country acquires more dollars that it needs in its working balances, it would have to present the excess for conversion into CRUs in the Reserve Settlement Account. The Federal Reserve Bank of New York, as agent for the United States, would buy and sell CRUs for dollars. Any country that needed dollars could get them for CRUs the same way it could get them for gold. All balance of payments settlements would be made in CRUs, the only final reserve asset. All transfers in CRUs, however, would be made on the books of the Reserve Settlement Account, run by the International Monetary Fund. That means that, in effect, when a country ran a deficit and settled in Composite Reserve Units, it would have reduced its ownership of gold, dollars, SDRs, in the proportion in which they were earmarked in the Reserve Settlement Account. In effect, it says, all different reserve assets must be used together in predetermined proportions. That prevented countries from using Gresham's Law--taking in gold and paying out dollars. And I set up tables to show how the Reserve Settlement Account would work. A country that had run a cumulative deficit would have reduced its balance in CRUs, and that meant an equal reduction in all of the different reserve assets it had earmarked. Because if it were to leave the Reserve Settlement Account (withdraw from it), it would get back the same proportion of the gold, dollars, etc., that it had deposited as its CRU balance was to its original opening balance.

S.B.: This is much the same principal that the European Monetary System is operating now.

Bernstein: That's right. They got the idea from my paper, the equal proportionate use of all reserve assets. Notice that while it's easy to say what a deficit country uses, what does a surplus country get? Of course, it has an increase in CRUs. That is equivalent to getting the different reserve assets in the proportion that they were earmarked by all the deficit countries. There's no distinction between surplus countries in what they get with the increase in their CRUs. Each deficit country had implicitly given up gold, dollars and other reserve assets in the proportion in which it had earmarked them. The total of the gold, of the dollar, and of other reserve assets given up by all the deficit countries was implicitly divided among the surplus countries in proportion to their surpluses. So surplus countries had no choice as to which assets they would accumulate. I first proposed the Reserve Settlement Account before the creation of SDRs. Later, after the SDRs had been allocated, I proposed that they also be deposited in the Reserve Settlement Account along with other reserves.

There was considerable interest in my proposal, but it had only limited support. Rasminsky, Governor of the Bank of Canada, thought it would be helpful, and O'Brien, Governor of the Bank of England, was very favorable toward it. Actually, it was a suggestion by Rasminsky that started me in this direction. During a discussion of reserves, he said to me, "Why don't you develop a system in which gold is in the system but nobody can try to grab all the gold." And that's what I did. I was in long correspondence with the French on this and I have a series of letters to and from Guillaume Guindey, an *Inspecteur des Finances*, elaborating the proposed Reserve Settlement Account.

The only time I proposed something like a substitution account was in December 1971. After the United States terminated the gold convertibility of the dollar, it accepted no responsibility for the dollar. What happened at the Smithsonian meeting in December 1971 is that the other Group of Ten countries were so eager to get the United States to fix a new parity, that they said to us, "You don't have to convert the dollar. We will support the dollar by buying all the dollars necessary to maintain the new par value." I didn't like that.

And so immediately after the Smithsonian meeting, I wrote a paper in which I recognized that the United States couldn't undertake the convertibility of the dollar because it could be drained of reserves, even if it had a surplus. That is because it could be running a surplus with countries that would settle in dollars, while it was running a deficit with countries that were gold holders and would want gold. My suggestion was that the United States should undertake to guarantee the SDR value of the net increment of dollars held by various countries. That means that it would be only the dollars that countries acquired from an aggregate U.S. deficit in the future that would be guaranteed. Unfortunately, that was a little too complicated. It would have been easier to understand if I had suggested that all official dollar holdings be guaranteed in SDRs. It would also have been a greater obligation than I wanted the United States to undertake then.

Well, after I wrote that paper I got a letter from Emminger of the Bundesbank saying, "What is the difference between your guaranteeing the SDR value of the dollar and our agreeing to take dollars to support the new par value?" The point that Emminger was making was that whether we assumed the risk of a fall in the value of the dollar or the Europeans assumed the risk, what was important was to have the foreign monetary authorities absorb the excess dollars representing the deficit on an official reserve basis. Arthur Burns, who is a friend of mine, invited me to the Federal Reserve to discuss the same question. He had Ralph Bryant with him, the director of international financial research.

I explained to Arthur Burns that if other countries have to support the dollar without any assurance of what it will be worth, then after they've accumulated a considerable amount of dollars, they're going to tell us they've tired of it. And we'll be confronted with a crisis. That's what I said to Burns. To Emminger I wrote and said, "If you guarantee the exchange rate for the dollar by accumulating dollars with no specified limit, the United States has no reason for trying to improve its balance of payments. It has a nice, cheap way to finance the deficit.

It's exactly what the French have said we are doing. You'll be doing it for us on a grand scale. But if we have to guarantee its value, then we aren't going to let the dollar depreciate, or it'll cost us more dollars." Nothing came of my suggestion. But I could see that we were running into all sorts of trouble.

Incidentally, in September 1971, I explained why the dollar had to be devalued, instead of having other currencies appreciated. I did this in a statement to the Joint Economic Committee, in which I said, if we expect the others to appreciate their currencies, then the aggregate currency value of reserves will be reduced. But if the dollar is devalued and other currencies revalued, the average currency value of aggregate reserves will either increase or be constant. I didn't see any sense in reducing the currency value of existing reserves.

The Fund then picked up this argument and the Treasury--which thought for a while it could get by without devaluing the dollar--became rather contemptuous of them. The Treasury was mad at the Fund anyway, for a variety of reasons. They said the Fund can't even rationalize it's own recommendations; they have to wait for Bernstein to tell them why they want the Treasury to devalue the dollar. At this time, in working with the Treasury, I ran into a problem that has confronted me many times, as the issuer of the EMB papers.

In May, 1971, I issued a paper called, "The Dollar is the Problem of the International Monetary System." In June, 1971, Edith and I went to an International Bankers Conference--only the billion dollar banks were invited--and I gave a paper there in which I said the dollar will have to be devalued. Actually the conference was opened with a speech by Emminger in which he said, "Bernstein says the dollar is the problem of the international monetary system. We agree," he said, "that this is a problem that we have to deal with."

S.B.: This was after the Mark had floated up.

Bernstein: Yes, and the Swiss franc had started up. That's right.

When I gave that speech and said the dollar would have to be devalued, Mr. Volcker answered me. He was the Undersecretary of the Treasury. I don't think he could persuade the bankers. In any case, it took a lot of boldness on my part to say this in front of all these people. The reporters were not allowed at the meetings, but they were briefed after the meetings. In the briefing, I didn't say a word about what I had recommended, so there was nothing in the newspapers about it.

I had issued a paper in which I said that any devaluation of the dollar would have to be done *de facto*; it couldn't be done *de jure*, the main reason being that it was necessary to have congressional approval for a change in par value, under the Bretton Woods Agreement Act. That's one of the things that couldn't be done without congressional approval. When I came back from Munich, the Treasury invited me to give a talk to the staff. Well, after I explained why I thought it was in our interest to devalue the dollar and not wait any longer--(we were multiplying all sorts of restrictions that were not working, but kept doubts about the dollar alive)--the Treasury economists began to ask me questions. And I could see from the questions, that what they had in mind was an import surcharge.

I went back to my office and started to write a paper in which I discussed the possibility of an import surcharge, in which case, we could tell what the Treasury was going to do. It would put the surcharge exclusively on manufactured goods, exempting goods from the developing countries, probably all commodities. After I had written the paper, I said to myself, "This isn't really fair. It isn't fair to have the Treasury invite me to come to a meeting, and let me discuss the need for devaluation of the dollar, have them ask me questions in good faith, trusting me to be on their side, and then announce to the world, before the Treasury did, the possibility of their imposing an import surcharge."

So what I did, in the end, was to write a paper in late July on the need for a *de facto* devaluation of the dollar.

S.B.: So, you were arguing against restrictive . . . or against a surcharge, and in favor of a general devaluation.

Bernstein: Yes. But more important, I didn't say the Treasury was going to impose a surcharge. I tore that piece up. The new paper (Brimmer told me) came up for discussion at the Federal Open Market Committee, because of its discussion of the impact the balance of payments had on employment. We did let the dollar depreciate *de facto* and at the end of 1971 we agreed with the Group of Ten on a new pattern of par values with a *de jure* devaluation of the dollar. Unfortunately this did not solve our payments problem.

In February, 1973, when I saw the problem becoming acute, I suggested that we do not devalue the dollar again. It didn't seem to me that it made much sense to keep devaluing the dollar when we weren't making any real progress in restoring our balance of payments. So, before the second devaluation, I wrote this letter on February 9th. Just read that paragraph.

S.B.: "Perhaps the present crisis can be overcome and, less likely, recurrent crises can be avoided. What is in question is whether it's worth the cost. If the signatories of the Smithsonian Agreement believe that exchange rates should be more flexible and parities adjusted more promptly, then this may be the time to apply these principles. The Smithsonian Agreement would remain in force. It would be desirable, however, to make two changes in the pattern of exchange rates. The first, to revalue the yen. Such an adjustment is not merely inevitable, it is indispensable now. The second is to allow the dollar to float temporarily by more than 2 1/4% below its parity. The countries in the Common Market would continue their cross-parities, and maintain exchange rates relative to each other."

Bernstein: Well, we didn't do that.

S.B.: Not in February.

Bernstein: Not until March. But there was always a lot more faith in the ability to make the new parities stick than I thought was desirable. I noticed a number of my papers discussed floating exchange rates very early.

S.B.: Well, the other thing about making a parity stick, is, of course, you have to have a domestic policy to back it up. And we weren't doing that at all.

Bernstein: That's the point. It was because I didn't see anything done between 1971 and 1973 and I wasn't that much frightened as to floating, that I wanted the dollar to float at that time. For one thing, I had written about it any number of times at the Fund. I always started these papers with the concept that the proper balance of payments--the one suited to the country--is based on the structure of the economy, on what you ordinarily generate in way of savings and domestic investment, and that it didn't make any difference in the trend balance of payments whether you have floating rates or fixed rates. All that floating did was to give a different time distribution of the surpluses and deficits over the cycle. I would have been willing to try this. I can't say that I think floating has worked very well since 1973 because even with floating rates, you have to follow policies that will maintain an appropriate balance of payments. One of my colleagues in England used to say that he wasn't against floating rates; he was against sinking rates. One of the difficulties, of course, is that you may even be less willing to follow such policies with floating rates than with fixed rates. Which has a greater disciplinary effect on domestic policy, a sinking exchange rate or a loss of reserves? It depends. In Europe, I'm sure sinking rates frighten everybody. They're accustomed to looking at the exchange rate. We're just learning to look at the exchange rates; we used to look at the gold reserves but it didn't seem to frighten us when the gold reserves fell.

To understand how difficult it would be to have fixed rates again we must look at the change in the structure of the U.S. balance of payments. Back in 1956, foreign investment began to revive. U.S. private capital outflow was $3 billion, foreign capital inflow was $2 billion, and the statistical discrepancy was $500 million. The inflow and outflow of capital was about 12 percent of exports and imports of goods and services. In the past four years (1980-83), U.S. private capital outflow averaged $83 billion a year, reported foreign capital inflow averaged $80 billion, and the statistical discrepancy averaged $23 billion, the net of very much larger gross capital movements. The inflow and outflow of capital in 1980-83 was about 27 percent of exports and imports of goods and services. That's to say, we now have an international financial system in which the payments which are sensitive to prices and incomes have become less important and those which are sensitive to interest, profits and capital gains have become more important. My opinion is that the big inflow of funds to the United States in 1980-84 came for profits and capital gains, not for higher interest rates. The catch phrase I use is that nobody pays fifty percent more in D-marks, for dollars, to earn four percent more per annum in dollars. But on the other hand, if you think the dollar is going to go up, it's a good idea to pay whatever the rate is. And if you think that the United States is going to be prosperous, then you will want to establish an affiliate here or buy stock in U.S. corporations.

And that's the problem now. If capital flows are going to remain so large relative to current transactions, can we have fixed rates of the kind established at Bretton Woods? On a typical day, the gross capital transactions in the exchange market may be four or five times as big as the current transactions. When we speak of a U.S. capital outflow of $55 billion in 1983 we mean the net increase in foreign assets owned by U.S. residents between the end of 1982 and the end of 1983. During the year they've been moving money back and forth on a much larger scale. And the net inflow of foreign funds has been even larger.

S.B.: Well, are there other things in the EMB period that we should touch on?

Bernstein: There may be. There were a lot of good papers on inflation.

S.B.: How about the commissions that you were involved with?

Bernstein: Yes. I was chairman of the commission for the balance of payments statistics, which was a mixture of academic and bank economists.

S.B.: Now, when was that?

Bernstein: That was printed in April of 1965, so it was probably appointed in 1964. The committee consisted of three professors--Caves of Harvard, Johnson of Chicago, and Kenen now at Princeton. And it had three bankers--George Garvy of the Federal Reserve Bank of New York, Walter Hoadley later of the Bank of America and Roy Reierson of Bankers Trust. We also had Charles Schwartz who was then at the International Monetary Fund and who was there presumably to make sure that our report fitted the views of the Fund on presenting the balance of payments.

I wrote a good many papers on inflation, including the concept of what is monetary stability. One of the papers I wrote was entitled, "Wages, Prices and Guide Posts." This paper was designed to explain what we are really after in the way of price stability.

S.B.: When was this? Roughly.

Bernstein: Around 1966.

S.B.: About the time of the Johnson administration?

Bernstein: Early in the Johnson administration. In this paper, I took up the question, which is it we want to stabilize?--consumer prices, wholesale prices, and if so, what part of the wholesale price index? I argued that, if you're thinking in terms of fixed exchange rates, then the consumer price index isn't the one you want to stabilize. I argued that it is the wholesale price index, excluding farm products and import goods. That would give you the best picture you could get of the price competitive position in internationally traded goods. And then I showed what this would mean. How much of the rise in the consumer price index was really due to services rather than commodities and so on.

Well, last February I had dinner with Paul Volcker. And he said to me that he thought that we were much nearer to price stability than people generally realized. So I said to him, what are you using for price stability? He said, "We're using your test." I said, "My test was the wholesale price index for domestically produced industrial goods." He said, "We're using the producer price index for finished goods excluding consumer foods and energy." So by excluding energy, I suppose, he really excluded the most important of the import goods.

I'm pretty sure that it was Henry Wallich that called the attention of the Federal Reserve to this definition. Actually, it's one of my earliest definitions. It goes back to the 1930s when I was teaching money at Chapel Hill. I spent a lot of time on theory of interest rates. I spent a lot of time opposing indexing. The paper I wrote on indexing was in my series. The American Enterprise Institute wanted to put out a pamphlet on indexing and it was a bit thin, so they were willing to pay me for the reprint rights to that paper. And I gladly sold it to them.

I would have said that also during this period, I was writing on the theory of money, interest rates, exchange rates. Probably one of my most successful papers was published at the Fund. This paper was entitled "Inflation and Development." It was actually a theory of inflation. This paper was reprinted so many times, that it must be the most widely reprinted of all the papers I wrote.

I first gave it, as a speech, at the University of Brazil in Rio--in English--and it was translated and published by them in Portuguese.

S.B.: When was that?

Bernstein: That was around 1952 when I was in Brazil. It had a lot of material in there that people borrowed and came to talk to me about. But they came in the 1970s and this paper was written in 1952.

The second version of this paper was part of a program at the University of Minnesota, printed by them in a book called, *Savings in the Modern Economy*, the theme of which is that it's lack of savings that makes inflation. And here is the way I looked at the problem. This paragraph will give you a concept of my views.

S.B.: "The ordinary functioning of an economy should result in distributing and using income in such a manner, that aggregate demand for output is equivalent to the cost of producing total output, including profits and taxes. At times, however, the government, businessmen or labor, may attempt to secure a larger part of the output than would accrue from the ordinary functioning of the economy. If other sectors are not prepared to acquiesce in this increase in the share of output used by any one sector, all the sectors together will be trying to get more of the national output than production has provided. This is the basic framework for the inflation process."

Bernstein: It then goes on later, to take up the point that in its initial aspect, the sector that wishes to get more will get it through credits and other ways. And that means, if you're not increasing output, it's a transfer from some other sector, probably consumption. Then, if labor acquiesces in it and says it's all right (especially if they get more employment too), then you simply have a higher level of prices once and for all, no further inflation, lower real wages for labor that it had expected or had before--though maybe more employment--and that'll be the end of it. But, if labor says, "No, we have to get back to what our traditional real wage is," then the inflation will continue unless you stop the sector that wants too much of the output. By that time, you may be generating a self-perpetuating inflation, where labor is the one that wants a larger share of the output than it could get under conditions of stability, perhaps justifying it as compensation for what it previously lost.

This paper was first published in English by the University of Minnesota; it was later published by the Fund; it was translated into French and published in Belgium; and then it was selected by the University of Chicago for printing in Spanish. The last one requires a little explaining.

The *Spanish Economic Review* had been suppressed under Franco. When Franco died and there was a return of liberalism in the country, they decided to revive the *Revista*. But they wanted to start with a selection of papers that had been published abroad that they wouldn't have had a chance to see, or comment on, and so on. And they asked the University of Chicago to pick the papers. The University of Chicago picked this as one of the papers. So it got into Spanish, too. That means it's been reprinted around five times that I know of.

S.B.: This is what is nowadays called: "The Competing Claims Theory of Inflation."

Bernstein: Well, of course, the money part comes in and somebody has to validate it. It also had other things in there. It was very widely used. In fact, I used it for a lecture at Chapel Hill. In the 1970s, Art Okun came to ask me what made me say in this paper, that inflation would lead to a shift in investment toward real estate, real property. I said that it wasn't anything in the theory that made me say it; it was what I saw them doing in Latin America. They were buying little bits and pieces of land; some of them only a few square yards. It was a paper that, in its pragmatic way, talked about what shifts would take place. And then, of course, it discussed the return to stability. I spoke of the possibility of cash crises, because if you don't let the money supply grow after you get stability, there could be a recession. And it is interesting to see how much greater the growth of the money supply has been since the virtual end of inflation.

S.B.: Is that in the EMB papers?

Bernstein: No. In any case, I've been following the change in M-1, and have been arguing that the big growth can be explained in two ways. First, the recent increase is a reversal of the reduction of cash balances relative to the gross national product that occurred during the rapid inflation. The rate of increase will slow of itself when the public has adjusted its holding of money to the appropriate relationship to an economy free of inflation. Second, the huge increase in M-1 has not been in currency or in demand deposits, but in other checkable deposits which bear interest--the NOW accounts. In large part, these accounts reflect a shift from savings deposits to other checkable deposits because differences in interest rates between the two types of deposits have become very small. If we had a different definition of M-1--say, non-interest-bearing deposits--then the growth of M-1 would not be excessive and the growth of M-2, which includes M-1, would be moderate compared to the trend rate.

S.B.: Very good. Thank you.

6

Epilogue: Reflections on the Fortieth Anniversary of the Bretton Woods Conference

by Edward M. Bernstein

The Founding of the Bretton Woods System[1]

The monetary history of the hundred years from 1873 to 1973 can be divided into three periods separated by two World Wars. The monetary system of each period was designed to correct the faults of the preceding period.

The first period, from 1873 to 1914, was the age of the classical gold standard, when all countries abandoned their silver or bimetallic standards to join the United Kingdom in a universal gold standard. More than half of this 40-year period is classified by the National Bureau of Economic Research as having been in the contraction phase of eleven business cycles. The classical gold standard broke down in World War I when all of the belligerents, except the United States, ended the gold convertibility of their currencies.

The second period was marked by the struggle to restore the gold standard in the 1920s and its abandonment by all countries in the Great Depression of the 1930s. Great wars breed great depressions and the first World War begot the greatest of all modern depressions. In the United States, the narrow money supply fell from $26.2 billion in June 1929 to $19.2 billion in June 1933, a reduction of 27 per cent. In these four years, the U.S. gross national product fell by 30 per cent in constant dollars and by 40 per cent in current dollars. The value of U.S. exports and imports both fell by two thirds, and by 1933 virtually all of the $7 billion of foreign bonds issues in the 1920s, as well as the Allied debts to the U.S. Government, were in default. Worst of all, the unemployment rate in this country soared from an annual average of 3.2 per cent in 1929 to 24.9 per cent in 1933. The depression in other countries was also severe, although not as bad as in the United States.

What caused the Great Depression? One view widely held abroad but also by some economists in this country was that the depression was the result of secular stagnation in the industrial world, particularly in the United States. This was not the view of the U.S. Treasury. We held that the Great Depression was caused by the interaction of the wartime inflation and the traditional gold standard. The war inflation exhausted the money-creating power of the gold standard world, and gold production after the war was not enough to sustain the growth of output at the higher postwar level of prices. Moreover, the restoration of the historical gold parity in the United Kingdom resulted in an overvaluation of the pound, while the establishment of a new gold parity in France based on a free market rate of exchange depressed by capital flight resulted in an undervaluation of the franc. The distortion of world trade caused by the misalignment of foreign exchange rates was aggravated by the high duties imposed by the United States under the Hawley-Smoot Tariff Act of 1930.

The Great Depression did not end until every country had abandoned the gold parity of its currency--the United Kingdom in 1931, the United States in 1933, and the gold bloc in 1936. To the countries that abandoned the gold parities, the consequent depreciation of their currencies was justified as a reasonable adjustment to their international economic position. To the countries that had not yet abandoned their gold parities, the depreciation of other currencies seemed to give those countries an unfair competitive advantage in world tarde. Changes in exchange rates must, by their nature, affect other countries; and they are, therefore, a legitimate matter of international cooperation. In his testimony before the Royal Commission on the Values of Gold and Silver, in 1887, Alfred Marshall made this reply to a question on the effect of the changes then taking place in monetary standards:

> "I think that there is a real, though very slow-moving, tendency for ...international interests to overrule national, and I think the time will come at which it will be thought as unreasonable for any country to regulate its currency without reference to other countries as it will be to have signalling codes at seas which take no account of the signalling codes at sea of other countries."

These were the problems, depression and the exchange system, that the 44 countries were concerned with at the Bretton Woods Conference in 1944. The United States was primarily interested in having stable exchange rates and orderly exchange arrangements. The countries that feared the recurrence of a great depression wanted the International Monetary Fund to have very large resources that its members could use to finance their balance of payments without resorting to measures that would restrict their own economies or the world economy. And I am reminded in a note from Emilio G. Collado, who was a technical adviser at Bretton Woods and the first U.S. Executive Director at the World Bank, that "the Latin Americans, and also the European countries that had suffered war destruction, made it clear that for them the establishment of the World Bank had priority."

It was much less difficult to reconcile these differences than one would have expected. The resources of the Fund were larger than the United States had originally proposed, and that made it more acceptable to other countries. At the same time, the Fund was given more authority over exchange arrangements than other countries had proposed, and that met the basic conditions the United States had set. Members of the Fund were required to establish a par value for their currency in terms of gold or the U.S. dollar. Changes in the par value could be made only if they were necessary to correct persistent balance of payments problems, and then only after consultation with the Fund and in most cases only with its approval. Members were also required to eliminate exchange restrictions on current transactions after a transition period. Members of the Fund could draw on its resources to supplement their own reserves in financing temporary balance of payments deficits, but they were expected to take measures to restore their payments position and to repay the Fund. That is the essence of what came to be called the Bretton Woods system.

The fear that the postwar world would be confronted by another Great Depression gradually abated. A related question, however, continued to trouble some economists--the fear of a chronic dollar shortage. They wanted the Fund to declare the dollar scarce. This would have allowed all countries to discriminate against the United States without violating the Fund Agreement. The European countries did have large current account deficits in the early postwar years which were mainly financed by the Marshall Plan. The view of the Fund as expressed by the Managing Director in an address at Harvard University in February 1948 was that "the shortage of dollars in Europe is very largely a reflection of the exceptionally great need for real resources in these countries. In part this may be a reflection of the phenomenon of inflation. Much more it is a reflection of the urgency felt by these countries to restore their economies much more quickly than they are capable of doing with their own output." As this implies, once the reconstruction of Europe was completed, the dollar shortage would come to an end.

The essential feature of the Bretton Woods system was its dependence on policies to maintain a well-balanced pattern of international payments and stable exchange rates. Under the gold standard, the settlement of balance of payments deficits and surpluses in gold brought about an automatic tightening of the monetary situation in the deficit country and an easing of the monetary situation in the surplus country that did restore the balance of payments after a time. It did not matter whether the deficit was caused by a cyclical expansion, where the gold outflow was a check to a too-easy monetary policy, or by a lasting change in a country's international economic position, in which case the gold outflow could restore the balance of payments only after a considerable fall in output and employment. This indiscriminate method of adjusting the balance of payments was accepted as an unavoidable aspect of the gold standard. Under the Bretton Woods system, however, balance of payments adjustments could be made though the appropriate policy--a restrictive monetary policy if the deficit was of a cyclical character, or a devaluation if there was an enduring deterioration in a country's international economic position.

As the exchange rate is a reciprocal relationship, it is affected not only by a country's own policies, but also by those of other countries. The gold standard set a limit to how far a country's monetary policy could depart from a norm set by the gold base for the money supply of the large trading countries, and this norm was not always conducive to maintaining high levels of output and employment. Under the Bretton Woods system, countries had to follow compatible monetary policies which were usually consistent with non-inflationary growth of their economies. As the dollar rate was regarded as the test of exchange stability, most countries followed monetary policies that were compatible with that of the United States. This aspect of the Bretton Woods system worked well as long as the United States had a balanced payments position and its prices and costs were reasonably stable.

Why did members of the Fund place so much emphasis on exchange stability? In part, no doubt, it was because of the tradition established under the gold standard. Mainly, it was because a fixed par value was conducive to economic growth with stability as long as the par value was appropriate to a country's international economic position. In the expansion phase of a cycle, part of the additional domestic demand could be met by an increase of imports of goods and services relative to exports, so that the effect of the excessive domestic demand on prices and costs was moderated. In the contraction phase of a cycle, the decline in domestic demand could be partly offset by an increase in exports relative to imports, so that the effect on output and employment was damped. As any one country was a relatively small part of the world economy--although this has to be qualified for the United States --it was not difficult for other countries to absorb such fluctuations imposed on their balance of payments provided they were not too large and were soon corrected.

This is how the Bretton Woods system worked for about twenty years. Output grew at the highest rate in modern times, not only in the United States, but even more in the other industrial countries and in many of the developing countries. The rapid growth of output was accompanied by an even greater increase in world trade and international investment. And this was achieved in an environment of unprecedented stability in economic activity. Not only was there no great postwar depression, but the cyclical recessions were much milder and shorter than in the past. According to the National Bureau of Economic Research, in the five cycles from 1945 to 1970, the average duration of the expansion phase was 50 months and the average duration of the contraction phase was 10 months. Moreover, there was a high degree of stability of prices and costs during much of this period, particularly from 1958 to 1965, when the U.S. wholesale price index of industrial goods was virtually unchanged and unit labor cost in manufacturing declined slightly. Unfortunately, after that the United States and other industrial countries had a continuous inflation of prices and costs.

Although a system of fixed par values has a stabilizing effect when the pattern of exchange rates is appropriate, it has a destabilizing effect when overvalued and undervalued currencies give rise to large and persistent deficits and surpluses. This happened when the United States had a persistent deficit on an official reserve basis from 1961 to the first quarter of 1973. In the earlier years the deficit was moderate and was due to the large increase in U.S. foreign investment. In 1971-72 the deficit became huge as a deterioration in the current account was superposed on a very much larger capital outflow. The U.S. deficit became a source of inflation in other industrial countries. Some of the output they needed for domestic consumption and investment went into increased exports to the United States; and the dollars and other reserves they acquired in settlement of their surpluses resulted in an expansion of the money supply far in excess of domestic needs. A realignment of par values at the end of 1971 did not restore the U.S. balance of payments; and in March 1973 the Bretton Woods system of fixed par values came to an end.

The decade of floating exchange rates has been marked by much greater inflation and much slower economic growth than at any time in the postwar period. In the United States, the implicit price deflator of the gross national product has risen by 120 per cent since 1972, the consumer price index has risen by 145 per cent, and the wholesale price index of industrial goods has risen by 174 per cent, much of it because of the sharp rise in energy prices. In a few countries the inflation was less than in the United States, in most countries it was considerably more. The growth of the real gross national product in the United States in 1972-83 was at about two-thirds of the rate in the preceding 25 years, and in the other industrial countries the growth of output slowed even more. In some developing countries, where production increased at very high rates until recently, the growth of output came to a halt in the past two years. The increase in the volume of world trade also slowed from 1972 to 1980, but then fell in the next two years, and the capital flow from the industrial countries to the developing countries has virtually stopped.

The slower growth and greater inflation were not mainly due to the abandonment of the Bretton Woods system. There were more important reasons for the poor performance of the world economy. Nevertheless, fluctuations in exchange rates have been much greater than would be expected from changes in relative prices and costs, and they have caused serious disruption in the world economy, particularly since mid-1980. In these four years, the foreign exchange value of the dollar has risen by an average of 65 per cent against the currencies of the Group of Ten and Switzerland, weighted by their global exports. The huge appreciation of the dollar was an important factor in slowing the inflation in the United States, but it caused an acceleration of the inflation in other industrial countries and impelled them to follow very restrictive monetary policies in order to avoid an even greater fall in the dollar exchange rates for their currencies.

The greatest effect of the appreciation of the dollar has been on the developing countries that are not members of OPEC. From late 1980 to late 1982, the International Monetary Fund index of dollar prices of basic commodities, excluding gold and oil, fell by 32 per cent. About half of the fall was due to the appreciation of the dollar and the rest to the worldwide recession. Since November 1982, the prices of basic commodities have recovered about half of the previous fall. In the meantime, the interest rates on their debts to the money center banks have risen sharply. As a consequence, they have had great difficulty in servicing their debts and they have had almost no access to bank credit. The International Monetary Fund is giving financial help to the heavily-indebted countries that adopt programs to slow the inflation and improve their balance of payments. Needless to say, the payments problems of the developing countries cannot be solved solely by belt-tightening. They need a renewed expansion of world trade, a further recovery in the prices of their export goods, and above all a reduction in interest rates.

The world economy would be better served if the large industrial countries assumed responsibility for maintaining greater stability in the exchange rates for the major currencies. There is no prospect, however, for the restoration of the Bretton Woods system, even with greater flexibility than in the past. Although the United States has made great progress in slowing the inflation, the sharp rise in the foreign exchange value of the dollar has made it very difficult for U.S. industries to compete in world markets. Moreover, the debt problems of Latin America have caused a serious deterioration in the U.S. trade position. The pattern of international payments is more unbalanced than at any time in the postwar period. It will remain that way until the surplus countries are once again willing to lend and invest their current account surpluses in the developing countries instead of pouring these funds into the very attractive money and capital markets of the United States. It would help too if the United States were less eager to absorb the inflow of foreign funds because of the deficiency in domestic saving as a result of the huge Federal budget deficit.

The most urgent task for the world economy, what is essential for maintaining a sound international monetary system, is to find a constructive solution to the debt problems of the developing countries. In this task, the lead will have to be taken by the two institutions established at Bretton Woods 40 years ago--the International Monetary Fund and the World Bank. We can be confident that they will be able to meet this responsibility if the debtor and creditor countries follow appropriate policies and if the high income countries provide these two institutions with the resources they need to do the job.

Bretton Woods and the Postwar Monetary System[2]

To those who had experience with the difficulty of getting international cooperation after World War I, the Bretton Woods Conference seemed like a miracle. The half dozen or more conferences on economic problems, monetary problems, and reparations problems from 1920 to 1933 accomplished nothing except the establishment of the Bank for International Settlements to deal with the transfer of reparations. By contrast, the Bretton Woods Conference achieved all that had been expected. The main reason was the thorough technical preparation which began more than two years before the conference. Another reason was that failure to agree on a monetary plan would have had a serious effect on Allied morale.

This does not mean that there was general agreement on what the postwar monetary problems would be. One widely held view was that the greatest problem was the danger of a recurrence of a deep depression in the United States. Those who held this view wanted the resources of the new institution to be very large, to expand steadily, and to be available automatically. They also wanted considerable freedom for countries to change exchange rates, to maintain exchange restrictions, and to postpone convertibility. When Lord Keynes wrote his proposal for a Clearing Union, he leaned to this pessimistic view of the postwar world. After Bretton Woods, however, Keynes came to believe that the dollar payments problem would be solved by expansion in the United States.

Harry White thought that the most important postwar problem was the threat of competitive exchange depreciation and discriminatory exchange controls, and they were the focus of his proposal for an International Stabilization Fund. He thought that Britain would quickly recover its capacity to produce and that the £4 billion of sterling balances accumulated during the war would give her an unfair advantage in exporting to the countries that held these balances. White also feared that Britain might devalue sterling and thus add to its competitive advantage in world export markets. After Bretton Woods he testified before the Senate Banking Committee that if the International Monetary Fund were established, Britain would need no help from the United States after the war. When I wrote the report of the Senate Banking Committee on Bretton Woods, I had the report say that the Committee did not agree with White's testimony and that Britain's need for a loan would have to be determined in the light of conditions at the end of the war.

Even within the U.S. technical group there were differences of opinion regarding the White Plan. At that time, many economists in this country held the view that the U.S. economy was doomed to stagnation and they preferred a bolder plan. Even Jacob Viner thought that the White Plan was too cautious. He described it as providing an umbrella when the world needed a bomb shelter. On the other hand, the Federal Reserve Board thought that the White Plan did not impose enough discipline. My notes on the meeting that White and I had with the Governors and staff contain this statement: "Mr. Gardner raised the question whether it wouldn't be desirable to require so much gold to be paid into the Fund that no country would have sufficient free gold to be able to disturb the international balance of payments without being subject to the discipline of the Fund." White and I also met with the directors and officers of the Federal Reserve Bank of New York where John Williams expressed the view that the White Plan had a too elaborate structure. He thought that the practical approach would be for Britain and the United States to agree on stabilizing the dollar/sterling exchange rate--the two key currencies. He later changed this, perhaps in response to our criticism, to the key-country approach.

The United States held discussions of the White Plan with 28 countries. The longest discussions, as would be expected, were with the British and covered both the White Plan and the Keynes Plan. The Canadians produced a proposal of their own to bridge the differences in the U.S. and British plans, with some new ideas not in either Plan. The Treasury amended the White Plan on the basis of these discussions to take account of the main concerns of other countries. Although we did not believe there would be a postwar depression or that the U.S. balance of payments would cause difficulties for other countries, we agreed to include a scarce currency provision in the White Plan. This would allow other countries to impose discriminatory restrictions against the United States if the dollar holdings of the Fund became scarce because of a depression in the United States. By these compromises we reached agreement on the main features of the new institution.

The agreement was put in the form of a Joint Statement of Experts on the Establishment of an International Monetary Fund. It covered the purposes and policies of the Fund, par values and changes in exchange rates, scarce currencies, and the transitional arrangements on exchange controls. These were principles for which detail would be provided by the Bretton Woods Conference. There is a wide range of detail that can be said to embody the same principle, so that there was plenty of work to be done at Bretton Woods. The Conference had two commissions, one on the Fund over which White presided, and the other on the Bank over which Keynes presided. The Fund Commission had four committees who considered the appropriate parts of the Joint Statement and relevant provisions submitted by the 44 countries.

The work went surprisingly well. There were a few technical questions that Commission I could not resolve and they were finally referred to a Special Committee on Unsettled Problems. The greatest credit, however, should go to the Drafting Committee which found the right words to reconcile lingering differences. At a dinner in Ottawa last year, I heard Governor Rasminsky, who was chairman of the committee, explain that there were no *unintentional* ambiguities in the Fund Agreement. It says much for the skill and tact of the Drafting Committee that there was universal satisfaction with the Articles of Agreement. Even Keynes, who had fought hard in the discussions with the United States to have the new institution in the form of the Clearing Union, stated in the House of Lords that "the new plan . . . [is] in some respects . . . a considerable improvement on either of its parents." The Fund Agreement that came out of Bretton Woods was simpler, clearer, and more workable than either the Keynes Plan or the White Plan.

I have sometimes wondered whether Keynes really wanted everything that he argued for in the Clearing Union. At a meeting in the Treasury in October 1943, Keynes announced that Britain was willing to accept the amended White Plan, but that he wanted to rewrite it in terms of bancor. If the British accepted the White Plan, I asked, what was the need to rewrite it. Because, Keynes replied with vehemence, "your plan is written in Cherokee." Later, in a speech in the House of Lords, Keynes said that with the new agreement "there is no longer any need for a new-fangled international monetary unit. Your Lordships will remember how little any of us liked the names proposed --bancor, unitas, dolphin, bezant, daric and heaven knows what." I think he would have liked SDRs but not the name.

I am not even sure that Keynes really wanted as large a fund as there would have been in the Clearing Union--about $30 billion initially and about $2,500 billion now. The initial sum was too large to let countries have unconditional access to such quotas. In the Clearing Union proposal, Keynes said that "there should be the least possible interference with internal national policies . . . [but] since such policies may have important repercussions in international relations they cannot be left out of account." He concluded that the proposed institution "should be limited to recommendations, or, at most, to imposing conditions for more extended enjoyment of the facilities with the institution offers." In a letter to me after the Conference, Keynes wrote: "I should like to see the Board of the Fund composed of cautious bankers, and the Board of the Bank of imaginative expansionists." Of course, he was talking about the cautious bankers of 1944, not those of 1984!

What was unique about the International Monetary Fund? The provision of reserve credit to central banks was not a novelty. The Bank of England had borrowed gold from the Bank of France and dollars from the Federal Reserve System in the past. The Bank for International Settlements made loans to central banks in the 1930s. And several writers had suggested in the 1930s that the deflationary effects of gold settlements could be avoided if surplus countries acquired foreign currencies rather than gold. Even the concept that exchange rates are a matter of international concern was not new. Marshall noted it in 1887, and the 1936 Tripartite Declaration of the United States, the United Kingdom and France, to which Belgium, the Netherlands, and Switzerland adhered, gave formal recognition to this principle.

What was novel in the Fund was the concept of a system of fixed but adjustable par values without the rigidity of the gold standard. There are numerous provisions on gold in the Fund Agreement, including the requirement that par values be stated in terms of gold as a common denominator or in the U.S. dollar of the gold content of 1944. Furthermore, to fulfill its obligation to maintain exchange stability under the Fund Agreement, the United States notified the Fund in 1946 that it would buy and sell gold freely for settlement of international transactions. These provisions were not enough, in my opinion, to make the Bretton Woods system a new form of the gold standard or the gold exchange standard.

In his speech in the House of Lords, Keynes said that the International Monetary Fund was the very opposite of a gold standard. "The gold standard, as I understand it," he said, "means a system under which the external value of a national currency is rigidly tied to a fixed quantity of gold which can only honourably be broken under *force majeure*; and it involves a financial policy which compels the internal value of the domestic currency to conform to this external value as fixed in terms of gold . . . [The Fund] Plan introduces in this respect an epoch-making innovation in an international institution, the object of which is to lay down sound and orthodox principles. For instead of maintaining the principle that the external value of a national currency should conform to a prescribed *de jure* external value, it provides that its external value should be altered if necessary so as to conform to whatever *de facto* internal value results from domestic policies."

In spite of the Gold Reserve Act of 1934, the United States was not really on a gold standard after 1933. The essence of the gold standard is that the money supply must be limited by the gold reserve. The last time that the Federal Reserve tightened its policy because the gold reserve ratio had fallen close to the legal minimum was on March 3, 1933, when the Federal Reserve Bank of New York raised the discount rate to 3-1/2 per cent. Thereafter, whenever the gold reserve neared the legal minimum, the required reserve ratio was reduced and finally eliminated. A country that loses more than half of its gold reserve, as the United States did in 1958-71, without reducing the money supply is not on the gold standard. What happened in August 1971 was the abandonment of the anomaly of convertibility of the dollar into gold when the United States was not on the gold standard.

If the Bretton Woods System was not a variant of the gold standard, how could exchange rates be expected to be stable? It was implicitly assumed that if the United States maintained reasonable stability of prices and costs, other countries would feel impelled to follow similar policies because of the emphasis they placed on maintaining the dollar exchange rates for their currencies. They could increase their reserves when they had an overall surplus, without depleting U.S. gold reserves, by acquiring part of the newly-mined gold that was not absorbed in the arts and industry, by adding to their official holdings of dollars, and by strengthening their net position in the Fund. They could finance overall deficits in their balance of payments through equal use of their own reserves and drawings on their Fund quotas. A trend change in a country's international payments position, however, would have to be met by changing the par value of its currency.

The Bretton Woods System did work more or less that way until 1957. At the end of that year, the gold reserves of the United States were about the same as they had been at the end of 1950. For the rest of the world, reserves had increased by about $500-600 million a year in official dollar holdings and by about $400-500 million a year in gold from current production and sales of the Soviet Union. The situation changed after 1957, but not because the United States failed to maintain stability of prices and costs. In fact, the 1958-65 period may have been the most stable in our history. The wholesale price index of industrial goods was virtually unchanged and unit labor costs in manufacturing declined slightly. The surplus on current account in 1961-65 averaged nearly $5 billion a year and was equal to 20 per cent of merchandise exports. The equivalent current account surplus now would be about $40 billion.

The U.S. payments problem was caused by the enormous increase in capital outflow. From 1951 to 1955, U.S. private foreign investment averaged less than $2 billion a year and was equal to 15 per cent of merchandise exports. U.S. foreign investment rose sharply after that. In 1961-65, it averaged $6 billion a year and was equal to 25 per cent of merchandise exports. In 1971-75, it averaged $23 billion a year and was equal to 31 per cent of merchandise exports. In the past five years, U.S. private foreign investment averaged $76 billion a year and was equal to

36 per cent of merchandise exports, although the figures are inflated by book transfers of the International Banking Facilities. It should be noted that in recent years the foreign capital inflow, including official funds and unrecorded transactions, was far in excess of U.S. private foreign investment.

The payments difficulties have been aggravated by the widespread and uneven inflation, by the huge increase in the cost of oil, and by the burden of debt in some of the developing countries. No system of fixed parities can function with such a pattern of international payments. The surpluses and deficits on an official reserve basis would have been far beyond the capacity of the monetary authorities to manage. Under the gold standard, they would have imposed an intolerable deflation in the deficit countries. With the Bretton Woods System, they would have caused an unacceptable monetary expansion in the surplus countries. With the present system of floating rates, the huge capital flows have not usually resulted in large overall surpluses and deficits; but they have caused wide fluctuations in the foreign exchange rates for the major currencies, most notably the enormous appreciation of the dollar since mid-1980. This has been very disturbing, particularly for the heavily-indebted developing countries; but it has not been accompanied by an exchange crisis, which would have been unavoidable with fixed par values.

What remains of the Bretton Woods system that was born here 40 years ago? The Fund is still the center for consultation and cooperation on international monetary problems, and it has been very helpful in dealing with the payments problems of some of its members. However, it has a much broader responsibility in connection with the present system of floating exchange rates. The second amendment to the Articles of Agreement, which formalized the end of the Bretton Woods System, states that "the Fund shall oversee the international monetary system in order to ensure its effective operation." I should like to see the Fund take a positive view of this responsibility. I hope this conference at Bretton Woods will help governments to understand the present problems and help the Fund to see what its role should be.

Bretton Woods and
Current International Monetary Problems[3]

The 40th anniversary of the Bretton Woods Conference is properly a time for viewing with pride the contributions of the International Monetary Fund to the functioning of the world economy. Although I am not an unbiased critic, I believe that the large increase in production and trade since the end of World War II was greatly facilitated by the international monetary system created at Bretton Woods. And I believe that in the past ten years, since the Bretton Woods system of fixed but adjustable par values broke down, the Fund has been indispensable in preventing the disintegration of the world economy.

This anniversary, however, should not be merely an occasion for congratulations, least of all from one who had the privilege of taking part in the Bretton Woods Conference and serving as the first director of research of the International Monetary Fund. The Fund has been entrusted with great responsibilities; and history will judge you not by what you accomplished in the past, but by how you meet the problems of the present and the future. And in this task, you can have no better guide than the Bretton Woods principles embodied in Article I of the Fund Agreement--the purpose of the International Monetary Fund.

The major purpose of the International Monetary Fund is to promote exchange stability and maintain orderly exchange arrangements among members. Bretton Woods is mainly associated with the exchange arrangements that were in effect from 1946 to 1973. There are other purposes, however, which reflect enduring principles to guide the Fund and its members. The first of these is that international monetary problems are matters of international concern. For that reason the Bretton Woods Conference established the Fund as a permanent institution for consultation and collaboration on international monetary problems.

The lesson that we seem to have to learn again and again is that there is no way by which a country can insulate itself from international monetary problems. That is because of their reciprocal relationship that is inherent in international trade and finance. The current account surplus of one country is the deficit of others. The capital inflow of one country is the capital outflow of others. The appreciation of one currency is the counterpart of the depreciation of others; and if the currency is the dollar, the change in its foreign exchange value will have a pervasive effect on the economy of all other countries. The problems of the heavily-indebted developing countries must inevitably affect the creditor countries, particularly the United States, their major partner in trade and finance. It is this reciprocal relationship that must be borne in mind by the Fund and its members in the measures they take to deal with the problems that confront them now and those that will inevitably arise in the future.

Unfortunately, countries sometimes ignore the international effects of their domestic policies, and they sometimes assume that they can shield themselves from the effects of the policies of other countries. The view so widely held a decade ago that floating exchange rates would provide automatic balance of payments adjustment and would give countries freedom in dealing with their domestic economic problems has proved to be exaggerated if not completely mistaken. If countries could ignore the composition of the balance of payments, it is obviously true that the balance on capital account will always equal, with the sign reversed, the balance on current account. And if countries were indifferent to the effects of large fluctuations in exchange rates on prices and output, then obviously the monetary authorities would be able to follow policies directed exclusively to their domestic economic problems.

It is paradoxical that a country may have less freedom in its monetary policy with floating exchange rates than under a system of par values properly related to each country's international economic position. That is because capital flows are greatly magnified with floating exchange rates. With an appropriate par value, a country could attract a capital inflow by a modest increase in interest rates when the exchange rate was at the bottom of the range. Capital came in from abroad to earn the higher interest rate and to profit from the recovery of the exchange rate. Once the currency reached the top of the range, however, the higher interest rate had much less effect in attracting a capital inflow as there was no possibility of a further rise and some risk of a fall in the exchange rate. With floating rates, an increase in interest rates also attracts a capital inflow; but far from being limited by the rise in the exchange rate, the capital inflow tends to increase because of the prospect of a further appreciation of the currency.

We have had a dramatic example of this in the past four years. Since mid-1980, the dollar has appreciated by an average of more than 65 per cent against the currencies of the Group of Ten and Switzerland weighted by their global exports in 1977-79. The rise in the foreign exchange value of the dollar was due to the capital inflow, and that was initiated by an increase in U.S. interest rates. The higher interest rates, however, cannot have been the main cause of such a huge appreciation of the dollar. There is no good economic reason for paying 65 per cent more for dollars in other major currencies merely to earn 3 or 4 per cent per annum more in the U.S. money market, particularly as the same rates are available in the Eurodollar market. There are other reasons why the capital inflow to the United States has continued on a massive scale, not the least of which is the expectation that the dollar will appreciate further. And because the appreciation of the dollar caused prices to rise in their currencies, other countries felt impelled to raise interest rates in their markets. That did not halt the capital outflow or the depreciation of their currencies, but it did impede their economic recovery.

The pattern of international payments is more distorted now than at any time in the history of the International Monetary Fund. One indication of the distortion is the enormous current account deficit of the United States which is being financed by a net capital inflow. Another, and more serious indication, is the severe payments difficulties of the heavily-indebted developing countries. Their difficulties are the result of mistaken policies, not only their own, but those of others as well. It would have been impossible for the debtor countries to have borrowed excessively unless the creditor countries had tacitly acquiesced in the lending of their banks by failing to restrain them. And the payments position of the debtor countries would not have deteriorated as much as it did if the industrial countries had not had the deepest recession of the postwar period, with a reduction in the volume of international trade, a fall in the prices of basic commodities, and an increase in interest rates. It should be added that the Fund is not without fault in failing to warn the debtor and creditor countries of the risks involved in such an enormous expansion of international bank loans. In an article published a few years ago, I wrote:

> The money-center banks will undoubtedly incur losses on some of their loans to the non-oil developing countries. The view that this will have a seriously disruptive effect on the international banking system is wholly unwarranted. Although the money-center banks will remain indispensable in helping to finance [their] deficits, much more of the financing will have to be done by official agencies, particularly the International Monetary Fund. Unless steps are taken to deal with the payments problems of the non-oil developing countries, the structure of the world economy will be weakened.

The actual situation is much worse than this projection; and the adjustment that the debtor and creditor countries will have to make will be more painful. One of the Bretton Woods principles is that adjustment of the balance of payments should be related to the cause of the payments problem. If the deficit, for example, is the result of excessive demand, then the proper remedy is to restrain domestic expenditure. But if the cause of the deficit is a cyclical change in international economic conditions, then the deficit should be financed by the use of reserves and credits until there is a recovery in the world economy. That is what the Fund Agreement means when it speaks of providing members with the "opportunity to correct maladjustments in their balance of payments without resorting to measures destructive of national or international prosperity."

The adjustment of the balance of payments of the heavily-indebted developing countries requires them to exercise great restraint in their economic policies. That is unavoidable. Even with very cautious policies, however, these countries will be unable to establish an acceptable balance of payments until there is a greater recovery in the volume of international trade, an improvement in their terms of trade, and lower interest rates on their debts to the money-center banks. In the meantime, these countries need a continued inflow of foreign capital on a moderate scale to enable them to work, to produce, and to trade. This is important to the creditor countries as well as the debtor countries.

The distortion in the U.S. balance of payments is to a large extent due to the payments difficulties of the heavily-indebted developing countries. Their inability to maintain their usual level of imports was a greater factor in the deterioration of the U.S. trade balance in 1981-83 than the appreciation of the dollar. Some of the foreign funds that came to the United States did so because the banks abroad, including the foreign offices of U.S. banks, did not regard it as prudent to continue their lending to the developing countries. It is difficult to see how there can be a significant improvement in the U.S. balance on current account or a considerable reduction in the net inflow of capital to the United States until the payments positions of the heavily-indebted developing countries are restored and they are once again accepted as creditworthy borrowers.

I have referred to the payments difficulties of the heavily-indebted developing countries and to the enormous appreciation in the foreign exchange value of the dollar not because I have suggestions for dealing with these problems, but to emphasize that there is no way by which a country can escape from the effects of national policies on the world economy. That is why the responsibilities of the International Monetary Fund are as great under the present system of floating rates as they were with par values. Some people believe that our present exchange and payments problems would not have arisen, at least not in the same acute form, if the par value system had not been abandoned. And a few people think that these problems would somehow disappear if only we restored the par value system. Their remedy for our problems is to hold a new Bretton Woods Conference.

The present exchange and payments problems were not caused by the abandonment of the par value system. It is more accurate to say that the collapse of the par value system in 1973 was due to changes in the world economy to which the United States and the other industrial countries were unable or unwilling to adjust their policies. Developments since then have made it even more difficult to restore a par value system. No system of fixed rates can function effectively under present conditions because of the worldwide inflation, the distorted pattern of international payments, the huge capital flows, and the misalignment of exchange rates. It would have been impossible for countries to accept the large transfers of reserves that would have been necessary to maintain stable exchange rates in the past few years. Nevertheless, such wide fluctuations in the dollar exchange rates for the major currencies could have been avoided. They were as much the consequence of national policies as of adverse developments in the world economy.

We do not need a new Bretton Woods Conference to devise new rules for achieving greater stability of exchange rates. The present Articles of Agreement give the International Monetary Fund adequate powers for surveillance of the international monetary system and for guiding the exchange rate policies of its members. At an appropriate time, the Fund could even determine that conditions are favorable for introducing a widespread system of stable but adjustable par values if this were to have the support of its members. That is not practical now, but the time may come when it will be feasible to have a somewhat greater degree of exchange stability in the international monetary system.

We cannot foresee when this will happen or what the new exchange system will be. There is a more critical attitude toward freely floating exchange rates and a more realistic view of the difficulties of maintaining stable exchange rates. Nevertheless, it would be futile to require the members of the International Monetary Fund to assume new obligations for maintaining exchange stability under present conditions. When the new exchange arrangements evolve they will probably combine a greater degree of stability than with floating rates and more flexibility than with fixed par values. A return to the gold standard in any form would impose too much rigidity on the world economy. As a practical matter, the new exchange arrangements will have to allow even more flexibility than the Bretton Woods system. Whatever the exchange arrangements may be, it will be necessary for the members of the Fund to follow policies conducive to stability of prices and costs, to adopt compatible monetary policies, and to collaborate in joint intervention to avoid excessive fluctuations in exchange rates. And we can be sure that in any new exchange arrangements, the Fund will still be carrying out the responsibilities entrusted to it by the Bretton Woods

Conference--to act as the center for consultation and collaboration on international monetary problems.

Notes

1. This paper was presented by Edward M. Bernstein at a celebration of the 40th Anniversary of the United Nations Monetary and Financial Conference of 1944. The celebration was held at the Mount Washington Hotel, Bretton Woods, New Hampshire, with a program entitled: "Bretton Woods Revisited, 1944-84."

2. This paper was presented by Edward M. Bernstein at a conference on "The International Monetary System: Forty Years After Bretton Woods," held at Bretton Woods, New Hamphire, May 18-20, 1984; and sponsored by the Federal Reserve Bank of Boston.

3. This paper was presented by Edward M. Bernstein at a luncheon meeting of the Executive Directors of the International Monetary Fund, July 26, 1984, to celebrate the 40th anniversary of the Bretton Woods Conference.

Glossary of Names

Acheson, Dean Gooderham (1893-1971) Assistant Secretary of State 1941-45,
Under Secretary of State 1945-47, Secretary of State 1949-53.

Alexander, Sidney (1916-) Economist, International Monetary Fund,
Professor, Massachusetts Institute of Technology, 1956-.

Berle, Adolph Augustus (1895-1971) Professor of Law, Columbia University
1927-64, Assistant Secretary of State 1934-38.

Bernhard, Arnold (1901-1987) Investment adviser, publisher. Chairman, Arnold
Bernhard & Co. Inc.

Blough, Roy (1901-) Economist, Director Tax Research, U.S. Treasury
Department 1938-46, Assistant to Secretary 1944-46, Member Council
Economic Advisers 1950-52, Professor International Business Columbia
University 1955-66.

Blum, Leon (1872-1950) Prime Minister and Finance Minister of France,
March-April, 1938.

Brimmer, Andrew (1926-) Economist and government official. Governor
Federal Reserve Board 1966-74.

Bryant, Ralph C. (1938-) Economist. Director, Division of International
Finance, Board of Governors of Federal Reserve System, 1972-75.

Bullock, Charles Jessie (1869-1941) Professor of economics Harvard, 1908-35,
Mem. Mass. Taxation Commission, 1907, Author, *Politics, Finances and
Consequences* (1939).

Burns, Arthur F. (1904-) Professor of Economics, Columbia University 1944-65.
Chairman, Council of Economic Advisers 1953-56. Chairman, Board of
Governors of Federal Reserve System 1970-78.

Carroll, Dudley Dewitt (1885-1971) Professor Economics, 1917-18, Dean, School
of Commerce, 1919-50, University of North Carolina.

Caves, Richard E. (1931-) Professor of Economics, Harvard University 1962- .

Coe, Frank (1907-80) Economist. Director Monetary Research, U. S. Treasury
Department Secretary of IMF, 1946.

Collado, Emilio Gabriel (1910-) Energy company executive. Economist
Federal Reserve Bank, 1936-38. Executive secretary Board of Economic
Operations, 1941-43. Chief division financial and monetary affairs 1944-45.
Director World Bank, 1946-47.

Cowden, Dudley (1899-1987) Professor of Economics & Statistics, 1935-72,
University of North Carolina.

Daniels, Jonathan Worth (1902-1981) Editor, Raleigh *News and Observer* 1933-42,
Executive editor, *News and Observer*, 1947, Editor *News and Observer* 1948-70,
Administrative Assistant to President 1943-45, Press Secretary to President
1945.

Day, Allan Charles Lynn (1924-) Professor of Economics, London School of Economics, Economic Adviser HM Treasury 1954-56.

Delmar, Alexander (1836-1926) Journalist, Financial Editor, *Hunt's Merchant Magazine,* Founder and editor from 1884-1866 of the *Social Science Review.* Director of U.S. Bureau of Statistics 1867-68. President of the Washington Statistical Society 1867.

Deming, Frederick L. (1912-) Banker. Federal Reserve Bank of St. Louis 1941-57. President, Federal Reserve Bank of Minneapolis 1957-65. Under Secretary for Monetary Affairs, U.S. Treasury 1965-69. General partner, Lazard Freres & Co. 1969-71. President, National City Bancorp., Minneapolis, 1971-82.

Dillon, Douglas C. (1909-) Director U.S. and Foreign Securities Corporation U.S. and International Securities Corporation 1937-53., President 1946-53. Under Secretary of State for Economic Affairs, 1958-59, Under Secretary of State, 1959-60, Secretary of Treasury, 1960-65.

Eckstein, Otto (1927-1984) Professor Economics Harvard 1955-84, Paul M. Warburg Professor economics 1975-84. President, Data Resources, Inc. 1969-81, Chairman, Data Resources, Inc. 1981-89. Author *The DRI Model of the U.S. Economy.*

Emminger, Otmar (1911-) German Banker. Bavarian Ministry of Economic Affairs, 1947-49. Board of Governors 1953-69, Deputy Governor 1970-77, Governor 1977-79, Deutsche Bundesbank. Executive Director IMF 1953-59, Governor, 1977-80.

Fisher, Irving (1867-1947) Professor Political economy, Yale University 1898-1935. Author: *Mathematical Investigations In the Theory of Value and Prices* 1892 *The Nature of Capital and Income, The Rate of Interest,* 1907, *The Theory of Interest,* 1930, and many others.

Fleming, J. Marcus (1912-1976) British Economist. Deputy Director, Research Dept., International Monetary Fund 1958-76.

Fowler, Henry H. (1908-) Investment banker. Economic advisor U.S. Mission, London, 1944. Special assistant to administrator Economic Cooperation Administration, 1945. Secretary of Treasury, 1965-68.

Frere, Maurice (1890-1970) Governor, National Bank of Belgium 1944-57. Chairman and President, Bank for International Settlements, 1946-58.

Friedman, Irving S. (1915-) International economist with Division of Monetary Research U.S. Treasury. Chief U.S. Canadian Division IMF 1946-48. Economic advisor to president IBRD 1964-72.

Friedman, Milton (1912-) Principal economist, Tax Division U.S. Treasury Department 1941-43. Professor of Economics, University of Chicago. 1948-62, Paul Snowden Russell Distinguished Service Professor Economics 1962-82. Author numerous books. Nobel Prize for Economics, 1976.

Galbraith, John Kenneth (1908-) Economist, Economic advisor National Defense Advisory Commission 1940-41, Deputy Administrator Office of Price Administration 1941-43. Professor Economics, Harvard University 1949-75, Paul M. Warburg professor economics 1959-75. Fellow, Trinity College, Cambridge University. Author of numerous books.

Garvy, George (1913-) Economic adviser, Federal Reserve Bank of New York.

Gilbert, Milton (1909-79) Economist. Chief National Income division 1941-1951. Director statistics and national accounts OEEC Paris 1951-75. Economic adviser Bank for International Settlements Basle 1975-79.

Graham, Frank Porter (1886-1972) President, University of North Carolina, 1930-49. UN Mediator, India and Pakistan. Chairman, National Advisory Council on Social Security.

Guindey, Guilluame (b.1909) Banker. Head foreign secretariat Algiers, Algeria, Paris 1943-53. General manager Bank for International Settlements, Basel, Switzerland 1958-63. Pres. Caisse Centrale de Cooperation Economique Paris 1965-72.

Gunter, John Wadsworth (1914-) Economist, Office International Finance, U. S. Treasury Department, 1941-48. Assistant Director Middle East Dept. IMF Washington, D. C.

Gutt, Camille (1884-1971) Business Executive, Brussels (Belgium). Minister of Finance 1934. Cabinet Member 1934-35. Minister of National Defense 1939-45. Minister for Economic Affairs 1940-45. Managing Director, International Monetary Fund 1946-51.

Haberler, Gottfried (1900-) Professor of Economics Harvard University, 1931-32, 36-71. Expert League of Nations Geneva 1934-36. Board of Governors Federal Reserve System 1943-44.

Harris, Seymour (1897-) Professor of Political Economy Harvard University 1922-64. Chief Economic Advisor to Secretary of the Treasury 1961-68.

Harrod, Sir Roy (1900-78) British Economist. Lecturer, Fellow, Christ Church College, Oxford University, 1922- . Advisor to International Monetary Fund 1952. President Royal Econonomic Society 1962-64.

Hawtrey, Ralph G. (1879-1971) Director of Financial Enquiries, H. M. Treasury, 1919-45. Professor International Economic Royal Institute of International Affairs, 1947-52. President Royal Economic Society 1946-48.

Hicks, Earl. (1916-1978) Economist. Director, Bureau of Statistics, International Monetary Fund 1968-77.

Hiss, Alger (1904-) Lawyer. President, Carnegie Foundation for International Peace. Director, Office of Special Political Affairs, U. S. State Department Convicted of perjury during McCarthy era.

Holzman, Franklyn (1918-) Economics Educator, Tufts University. Economist U.S. Treasury 1947-48, Consultant 1949-52.

House, Robert B. (1892-1987) Dean of Administration, University of North Carolina, 1934-45, Chancellor 1945-57.

Jacobsson, Per (1894-1963) Managing Director, International Monetary Fund 1956-63. Economic Advisor and Head of Economic Department Bank for International Settlements, Basel 1931-56.

Johnson, Harry G. (1923-79) Canadian economist. Professor of Economics University of Chicago 1959-79, London School of Economics 1966-74. Editor, *Journal of Political Economy* 1960-66, 71.

Kenen, Peter B. (1932-) Economist, educator. Professor of Economics Columbia University 1964-71. Walker Professor Princeton University 1971- . Advisor U.S. Treasury 1962- .

Keynes, John Maynard (1883-1946) Editor *Economic Journal* 1911-44. Lecturer King's College Cambridge 1908-42. Principal Treasury Representative at Paris peace conference 1919. Member Commmittee on Finance and Industry 1929-31. Author, *General Theory of Employment, Interest, and Money* (1936) and many others. Director Bank of England.

Kondratieff, Nicholas D. (1892-?) Russian economist. Director, Moscow Business Conditions Institute, 1920-28. Author, *Major Economic Cycles*, 1928. Imprisoned and died in the 1930s.

Lange, Oskar (1904-65) Economist, Professor of Economics at The University of Chicago 1943-45. Professor University of Warsaw 1955-65.

Marshall, Alfred (1842-1924) Professor of Political Economy, Cambridge U. 1885-1908. Author, *Principles of Economics, Money, Credit, and Commerce.*

Martin, William McChesney, Jr. (1906-) Banker. A. G. Edwards & Sons, St. Louis 1929-38. Chairman, New York Stock Exchange 1938-41. Chairman, Export-Import Bank 1946-49, Chairman, Federal Reserve Board, 1951-69.

Meade, James Edward (1907 -) Professor of Political Economy, Cambridge 1957-68. Economic Section of League of Nations Geneva 1938-47 Director (1946-47). Nobel Prize for Economics 1977.

Millis, Harry Alvin (1873-1948) Professor of Economics 1916-48, Chairman 1928-38, University of Chicago. Labor economist.

Mitterand, Francois (1916-) First Secretary Socialist Party 1971-81. Secretary General Organization for Prisoners of War and Refugees 1944-46. President of France, 1981- .

Model, Leo (1904-) Internat. Economist. Internat. banking business Holland 1935-41. Model and Roland, NY Stock Exchange 1941- .

Monnet, Jean (1978-79) European political figure. Created Plan Monnet 1946. General Counsel Plan for Modernization and Equipment of France 1946.

Morgenthau, Henry, Jr. (1891-1967) Secretary of Treasury, 1934-45.

Murchison, Claudius Temple (1889-1968) Professor of Economics, University of North Carolina, 1921-34. Director U.S. Bureau Foreign and Domestic Commerce, 1934-35. President Cotton Textile Institute, 1935-49.

O'Brien, Sir Leslie (1908-) Bank of England 1927-73, Governor 1966-73.

Okun, Arthur (1928-1980) Economist, Member (1964-68), Chairman, Council of Economic Advisors, 1968-69. Professor of Economics at Yale 1963-64. Senior Fellow, Brookings Institution, 1969-80.

Opie, Redvers (1900-) English economist. Senior Fellow Brookings Institution 1947-53. Economic Advisor British Embassy in Washington 1939-46. Fellow, Lecturer, Magdalen College Oxford U. 1931-39. Economic Counsellor American Chamber of Commerce of Mexico 1966.

Paish, Frank Walter (1898-) Professor of Economics. London School of Economics 1949-65.

Patterson, Gardner (1916-) Professor Princeton 1955-69. Director International Finance Section 1949-58. Dean, Woodrow Wilson School of Public & International Affairs. Deputy Director, GATT 1969-80.

Penzias, Arno (1933-) Astrophysicist. Research scientist, Director research, Bell Labs 1976-79. Manager Editorial Board AT&T Bell Labs Technical Journal 1978-84. Recipient Nobel Prize for Physics.

Phillips, Sir Frederick (1884-1943) Second Secretary, HM Treasury. Chairman of the Financial Committee of the League of Nations. Representative H.M. Treasury in Washington, 1940-1943.

Pigou, Arthur C. (1877-1959) Professor of Political Economy Cambridge 1908-43. Member of Committee on Currency and Foreign Exchange 1918. Author, *Economics of Welfare.*

Playfair, Sir Edward (1909-) HM Treasury 1934-46, 1947-56. Permanent Under Secretary of War 1956-59, Permanent Secretary of Defence 1960-61.

Polak, Jacques T. (1914-) Economist, IMF. Deputy Director Research Department 1952-58. Director of Research Department 1958-79. Economic Counsellor 1966-79. Executive Director, 1981.

Rasminsky, Louis (1908-) Canadian banker. Executive Assistant to Governor of Bank of Canada 1943-54. Deputy Governor Bank of Canada 1956-61. Member Canadian delegation to Bretton Woos Conference 1944 and to San Francisco Conference of UN 1945. Executive Director of IMF 1946-62.

Robertson, Dennis H. (1890-1963) Professor of Political Economy, University of Cambridge 1944-57. Adviser, H.M. Treasury 1939-46. President of Royal Economic Society 1948-50.

Roosa, Robert (1918-) Federal Reserve Bank of NY, 1946-1960. Under Secretary for Monetary Affairs, U.S. Treasury 1961-64.

Rooth, Ivar (1888-1972) Governor, Central Bank of Sweden 1929-48. Managing Director, International Monetary Fund 1951-56.

Samuelson, Paul A. (1915-) Economics educator. Consultant U.S. Treasury 1945-52, 1961-69. Professor of Economics M.I.T. 1940- . Author, *Foundations of Economic Analysis* 1947 and many others. Nobel prize in Economics, 1970.

Schumpeter, Joseph Alois (1883-1950) Austrian Minister of Finance 1919-20. Professor of Economics, University of Bonn 1925-32. Professor of Economics, Harvard 1932-50. Author, *Capitalism, Socialism, and Democracy.*

Shea, Francis Michael (1905-) Chairman Attorney General's Commission on Bankruptcy Administration 1941-45.

Shoup, Carl Sumner (1902-) Professor Economics Columbia University 1928-71. Assistant to Secretary of Treasury 1937-38. Consultant 1938-46, 1962-68. President, International Institute of Public Finance. Author of numerous books.

Smith, Adam (1723-1790) Professor of Moral Philosophy University of Glasgow 1752-63. Author, *Wealth of Nations* 1776. Commissioner of Customs, Scotland 1778-90.

Snyder, Carl (1869-1946) Statistician, author. President American Statistics Association 1928. Author, *Capitalism the Creator: The Economic Foundations of Modern Industrial Society.*

Southard, Frank Allan, Jr. (1907-) Economist. Chairman, Department of Economics, Cornell University 1946-48. Director Office International Finance US Treasury 1947-48. U.S. Executive Director IMF, Special Assistant to Secretary of Treasury 1949-62.

Spruill, Corydon P. (1899-1988) Economist, Professor of Economics University of North Carolina 1932-68. Dean of Faculty 1955-57.

Taussig, Frank W. (1859-1940) Henry Lee Professor of Economics, Harvard University 1901-1935. Chairman U.S. Tariff Commission 1917-19. Editor, *Quarterly Journal of Economics* 1896-1937.

Thorp, Willard L. (1899-) Economist. Professor, Amherst College 1926-33. Chief economist, Dun & Bradstreet 1935-40. Assistant secretary economic affairs, U.S. Department of State, 1946-52.

Tooke, Thomas (1774-1858) Engaged in the Russian trade in London. Author, *Thoughts and Details on the High and Low Prices of the 30 Years from 1793 to 1822* (1823).

Triffin, Robert (1911-) Director, Exchange Control Division, IMF 1946-48. IMF Representative for OEEC Payments Commission, Paris, 1948-49. Professor of Economics, Yale University 1951-80. Professor, Louvain University 1980- .

Varvaressos, Kyriakos (1884 -1957) Economist, Ambassador for economic affairs representing Greece at Bretton Woods 1944, San Francisco 1945. Executive Director IBRD since May 1946.

Villard, Oswald Garrison (1872-1949) Journalist. Editor and owner NY *Nation* 1918-1932, Publisher and Contributing editor 1932-35. Author *Free Trade-Free World.*

Viner, Jacob (1892-1970) Professor, University of Chicago, 1916-46. Professor of Economics, Princeton University (1946-60). Professor Emeritus 1960-70. Taussig visiting research professor, Harvard 1961-62. Consultant United States Treasury 1935-39. Consultant U.S. Department for State 1943-52. Author, *Studies in the Theory of International Trade, The Customs Union Issue, International Economics.*

Vinson, Frederick Moore (1890-1953) Mem. Congress 1923-29, 1931-38. Associate Justice, U.S. Court of Appeals 1938-43. Director, Office of Economic Stabilization 1943-45. Secretary of Treasury 1945-46. Chief Justice, U.S. Supreme Court 1946-53.

Volcker, Paul A. (1927-) American banker and government official. Special Assistant Securities Department Federal Reserve Bank of New York, 1953-57. U.S. Treasury Dept. 1962-63. President New York Federal Reserve Bank 1975-79. Chairman, Board of Governors Federal Reserve System 1979-87.

Wallich, Henry (1914-87) Federal Reserve Bank of New York 1941-51. Prof. of Economics Yale University, 1951-74. Member, Federal Reserve Board of Governors, 1974-86.

White, Harry Dexter (? - 1948) Assistant Director of Research, U.S. Treasury 1934, Director Monetary Research, U.S. Treasury 1935-44, Assistant Secretary of Treasury 1945-46. U.S. Executive Director, IMF 1946-47.

Wolf, Harry D. (1895-1960) Ph. D. 1926 University of Chicago. Associate professor 1928-36, Professor 1936-60, University of North Carolina.

Woosley, John Brooks (1892-1956) Ph. D. 1931 University of Chicago. Associate professor 1924-29, Professor 1930-56, University of North Carolina.

Zimmermann, Erich Walter (1889-1966) Professor of Economics, University of North Carolina, 1922-41. Author, *World Resources and Industries* (1933). Member, Inter-University Committee, National Bureau of Economic Research.

About the Book and Author

This book consists of a set of conversations with Edward Bernstein, whose long life has taken him from his student days at Chicago and Harvard in the 1920s to his present-day role, at the age of 86, as an active analyst of monetary affairs. In between, he has been a college professor, principal economist at the Treasury Department during World War II, chief technical adviser and spokesman for the U.S. delegation at Bretton Woods, and head of research for the International Monetary Fund.

Few economists besides Bernstein have been as closely involved with important twentieth-century monetary events. This volume of reminiscences, in the form of interviews conducted by Stanley Black, reveals Bernstein to be a talented and poignant story teller as well. His reflections are a treasure trove of anecdotes and inside stories of his dealings with Keynes, Friedman, Acheson, Harry Dexter White, and many others. Especially valuable are his accounts of the Bretton Woods Conference, including its background, the preparations for it, and its aftermath.

Professor Black succeeds admirably in drawing out both the drama and the pleasures of an important public life, a life lived with wit and vigor. Bernstein's story is a valuable document for monetary historians as well as for students of twentieth-century economics.

Stanley W. Black is professor of economics at the University of North Carolina–Chapel Hill.

Index